ROSICRUCIAN PRINCIPLES
FOR THE
HOME AND BUSINESS

▽

Rosicrucian Principles

for the
Home and Business

By H. SPENCER LEWIS, PH.D.

AMORC

Published by the Grand Lodge of the English Language Jurisdiction, AMORC, Inc.

First Hardbound Edition, 1929

©1929, 1953, and 1981 by Supreme Grand Lodge of
AMORC, Inc.
All Rights Reserved

ISBN 0-912057-04-1

©1995, Supreme Grand Lodge of the Ancient & Mystical Order
Rosae Crucis. Published by the Grand Lodge of the English
Language Jurisdiction, AMORC, Inc.

Library of Congress Catalog Card No.: 54-21694

First Paperbound Edition, 1987
ISBN 0-912057-54-8

10 9 8 7 6 5 4 3

Printed and Bound in U.S.A.

DEDICATED

*to the student of all natural and
spiritual laws who remembers
that the Great Master
Jesus taught the first
lessons in the art of
living a practical
and useful life
a m o n g
men.*

▽

The Rosicrucian Library

(Other volumes will be added from time to time.
Write for complete catalogue.)

Contents

▽

Introduction

▽

Soon after the re-establishment of the Rosicrucian Order in America for its present cycle, hundreds of the members petitioned the Supreme Officers for special information relative to the application of the Rosicrucian principles to business affairs.

Rosicrucianism, as presented by the AMORC in America and other lands today, is a practical philosophy, *a science of demonstrable laws*. The Rosicrucians were always practical men and women, laboring with nature's laws for the sole purpose of improving their own, and others' lives here on earth, *now*. Hence the Rosicrucians had naught to do with speculative philosophies, hypothetical problems, and fantastic theories. They worked in their laboratories, solving the chemical and physical mysteries of the material world as well as concentrating in their sanctums on the development of their personal, latent, dormant faculties.

According to the Rosicrucian standard of living, each man and woman should attempt, by every means that is ethical, moral, and Cosmically approved, to succeed in life, enjoy health, happiness, the material luxuries, and the comforts of physical existence as well as seek to attain spiritual Peace and attunement. In fact, the Rosicrucians have ever held that truly to fulfill the mission of our existence here on earth, and thereby carry out the Divine Will, no man and no woman should slight or negate the material or worldly obligations which are incumbent upon all of us, but each should *master them,* meet them, and make an eminent success of his or her earthly career. This, say the Rosicrucians, will bring one more truly in contact with the universal laws of nature and attune one more consciously with the universal scheme of things than living a life of speculative abstraction or spiritual monasticism.

Every one of the Masters of the Great White Brotherhood has devoted the larger part of his earthly life to the application of his knowledge for the alleviation of suffering, the advancement of learning, the promulgation of science, and the achievement of worldly happiness and prosperity. Each has contributed to these elements of our life by and through intimate contact with the problems of our existence and association with men and women struggling to live an exemplary life of a "light on earth." None ever lost the human touch, the companionship with his earthly brethren, nor the opportunity to work out, in a material way, the solution to man's actual physical problems.

It is but natural, therefore, that students of the Rosicrucian teachings would become imbued with this practical standard of living, and seek more information relating to the solution of their personal problems. The organization expected—and even anticipated—this, and glories in the fact that with all the schools of speculative, abstract, *impractical* philosophies operating today, the Rosicrucian Order once again shows its unique and distinct place in the lives of humans by meeting a demand more important and more useful in the pursuit of health, happiness, and Peace than any other.

Among the most important problems facing men and women today are those which relate to success or prosperity in the business world. Success in such matters does not always mean the attainment of *great wealth*, although this is neither impossible nor undesirable; nor does success and prosperity in business necessarily indicate a selfish heart and a greedy motive.

Most men and women in the business world to-day—especially those who are of the type and mind to become students of the Rosicrucian teachings—are in business because they enjoy its activities, seeking to contribute to the world's progress, and desiring to meet their obligations, fulfilling their duties, carrying on what seems to be their mission in life, and enjoying sufficient prosperity to be able to help others as well as help themselves. Surely, no higher motive can actuate any being in any endeavor or aspiration.

These persons deserve to succeed, for their success and prosperity in the business world will help business generally and will bring happiness and Peace to others. For this reason the Rosicrucian Order realizes its own duty and obligation, and is happy to aid and guide, to the best of its ability, its members and friends in attaining success in business matters.

For the Home and Business

With men and women well trained in the special application of Rosicrucian principles to business problems, it has been possible to advise and aid thousands who have attested to their increasing success, and affirmed their debt of gratitude to AMORC.

Introducing the Author

∇

Many years ago the Imperator of the AMORC for North America was selected by prominent business men in New York and other cities as their adviser in special matters. His unusual ability to sense conditions intuitively, his ready contact with the minds of others and with the universal mind of the masses, plus his strange ability to direct, or engineer, the successful issue of the most involved and difficult plans, attracted the attention of many men of large affairs. He soon became the "silent partner" in many corporations and organizations, accepting only donations toward the great work of AMORC as his compensation. In whatever city he traveled in behalf of the work of AMORC he was sought by business men and women for short consultations, and it became notable that whenever Dr. H. Spencer Lewis gave his approval to a plan and said that he would use his "methods" to bring the matter to a conclusion, *there was eminent success.*

After a number of Better Business Bureaus, Boards of Trade, Business Guilds, Clubs and

Societies had invited Dr. Lewis to speak at their weekly or monthly sessions, he was importuned to prepare a series of weekly talks to be delivered to one of the largest classes of business men and women ever called together to hear a man speak on the mystical principles involved in "good business." These lectures enabled the attendants to achieve such unusual success in their personal affairs that the reports of the results spread from city to city, from one business man to another.

Many hundreds of requests have been received weekly from all parts of the United States asking that the original lectures given by Dr. Lewis be reproduced. Business magazines offered to publish them serially, and book publishers likewise offered good sums for the exclusive right to commercialize them.

It was decided, however, by the Imperator himself, that the plan suggested by the Supreme Secretary was more in keeping with the ideals of AMORC and that instead of permitting any publishers to issue and sell these lecture lessons at a great profit as a commercial venture, the "Business Advisory Bureau" of AMORC should issue the matter in a small book to sell at a reasonable price with a nominal profit, which profit could be used by AMORC in its various welfare activities.

The present book is the result of this decision. The original lectures given by Dr. Lewis have been augmented, revised, and extended. None of the secret teachings of the Rosicrucian Order is presented in its fullness, but every mystical method is utilized. Therefore this book can be used by members of the Order or their friends.

We would remind each reader of this book that the complete teachings and full work of AMORC are not represented by the few laws and principles applied in the lectures given in the following chapters. In fact, the principles and formulas used for the lessons in this book were extracted from the hundreds of lessons of the AMORC which deal with scores of other vital matters, such as the development of latent abilities, the awakening of dormant talents, and the building up of such functions as intuition, mental creation, healing powers, Cosmic attunement, prophecy, and other powers which enable men and women to master their lives and succeed in being healthy, prosperous, and happy. Such complete instruction is given freely to those who are members of the organization, but cannot be published in books for public circulation.

Readers Please Note . . .

Rosicrucian Principles for the Home and Business was first published in 1929, just before the onset of the Great Depression. This book reflects the realities of the business world at that time, when most businesses were owned and controlled by men. As a result, a majority of the case studies describe the experiences of men and only rarely touch upon the experiences of women.

Nevertheless, the metaphysical principles explained in this book are as applicable in today's business environment as they were during the author's lifetime. We encourage you to read this book with an open mind, and to focus on the general principles rather than on certain dated references. Whether you are a man or a woman, you can apply these timeless techniques in your own life to bring about greater success and happiness today.

—The Editors

CHAPTER I

THE TRUTH ABOUT AFFIRMATIONS

HE late French psychologist, Coué, did not introduce anything new into the American popular misunderstanding of psychological principles when he promulgated his prettily worded affirmation, "Every day in every way I am getting better and better."

In the Occidental world generally, the value or usefulness of affirmations to affect one's physical, mental, or material conditions has been greatly misunderstood, and the same may be said of the real fundamentals of applied psychology.

The Orientals, long familiar with the mystical laws of life, are quite aware of the fact that the mere affirmation of *wealth* or *health* will not bring these desirable things into the environment where they do not exist. The real mystics of every land, and especially those who have been thoroughly trained in the Rosicrucian principles, know that certain affirmations under certain conditions have some value and a real place in the scheme of things, but they also know that an *untrue* or *unsound* affirmation is not only valueless, but really detrimental.

How can the affirmation: "I am in perfect health and in complete attunement with God," have any effect upon the physical condition of a person who, at the very moment of making the affirmation, is suffering from pain, due to some diseased or abnormal condition?

Pain, as we shall see later on in another chapter, is not something that should be affirmed out of existence as a condition unwarranted by nature and unauthorized by God. It is one of God's own creations and a perfectly natural thing when the body is diseased, or in some abnormal physical or mental condition. Pain always has a cause for its existence, and a reason for its manifestation. The cause may be unnatural; it generally is unnecessary. But pain as a result of disease is perfectly logical, natural, and a Divinely authorized principle. To affirm, therefore, that one has no pain when pain is quite manifest, is attempting to deny the existence of something that not only logically exists, but which has a good purpose for its existence, and a motive which will serve us and help us if we but realize it. Therefore, not pain, but the *cause* of the pain should be considered as the undesirable condition to be relieved.

But disease, or any abnormal condition of the mind or body, cannot be relieved by affirming its non-existence.

Poverty and failure in business and material affairs cannot be altered by the affirmation that these conditions do not exist, and are only imaginary things, to be swept out of the consciousness and cleansed out of the mind by a denial that they are there.

For a man or women who seeks relief from debt and solicits the Cosmic aid in having an abundant supply of necessities, to affirm that "I am not in debt, and I have the riches of the Cosmic at my disposal," is merely to attempt to blind the consciousness to the existing conditions, and to so charm the objective mind by a false picture of imaginary conditions that, for the time being, all effort to relieve the situation in the proper way is cast aside. In this attitude of self-induced hysteria, one can believe that all is well and that there is no need for effort or even thought in any other direction.

The man or women who has become an addict to the drug habit, and who shuts out the worries, trials, and problems of the hour by the induction of sleep, or the stimulus of a flighty imagination, with glorious pictures of wealth and contentment, is no less a victim to a false practice than the one who affirms the non-existence of real conditions and proclaims the actual existence of imaginary bounties.

As may be judged by the foregoing remarks, the mystic who is really familiar with the laws of Nature and the operation of the Cosmic methods, knows that his dominion over his affairs and the use of his *will* to regulate his conditions, must be directed toward changing *causes* of conditions rather than denying the *manifestations* of the causes.

The misunderstanding regarding affirmations came about through a miscomprehension of the Oriental and mystical conceptions of the fundamental laws of psychological consciousness.

The real mystic knows that it is wrong and unsound to admit outwardly or inwardly the existence of a condition which is not real. He will not admit that he must continue to suffer pain or suffer from disease or suffer from poverty or the lack of necessities. He will even go so far as to deny these things the power to enslave him. He is quite positive in his negation of the omnipotent power assigned to material things of his earth life to control his living and to limit the enjoyment of the Cosmic blessings.

But the mystic denies these things and rules them out of his life, not by affirming that the manifestations do not exist, but by affirming that these things shall not continue to be and are not what they seem to be, and must submit to his will.

In later chapters, we shall see that just as pain is a natural result of a cause, so poverty and a lack of the necessary things, or even the luxuries of life, are a result of a cause, and the cause must be affected.

When one suffers from the agonizing pains of toothache, it is indeed foolhardy and entirely inconsistent with Cosmic and natural law to affirm:

"I have no toothache, and am at peace with the universe." Such an affirmation neither affects the toothache as a pain, the cause of the toothache and its pain, nor anything else concerned therewith. Nor does it bring about any substantiating proof that the sufferer is, at the time, at peace with the universe. The practical mystic—who does not dwell in the clouds of hypothetical postulations and ethereal speculations based upon theories discovered by eminent founders of new schools of psychology—knows that he must direct the use of his will power, and the magnificent creative forces of his mind, to the immediate alteration of the condition which is the real cause of the pain in the tooth. Thereby he relieves the pain without giving it any undue consideration in a negative sense.

The mystic thus informed brings his suffering to an end, and quickly demonstrates that he can be "at peace with the universe," and truly is "a child of God's love," by re-establishing the harmonium in his body through the removal of the cause of disease and suffering.

The man or woman who is without the immediate necessities to meet a material emergency of either a financial or any other form, will find that the affirmation of "I need have no concern, for the abundant supply is mine," brings no relief and simply inhibits as well as prohibits such action on the part of the individual as would actually bring about the desired relief.

In the following chapters of this book—which are really specific and practical lessons in the application of certain mystical laws—the correct use of the proper affirmations will be explained. It is the purpose of this preliminary lesson to remove from your mind the misunderstanding and the misconception that may exist regarding affirmations as generally promulgated by popular lecturers, who are generally less informed regarding the mystical laws of the universe than they are about the superstitious beliefs of a multitude of persons, who think that a few lessons in psychology will furnish the key to the mastership of all of life's problems.

Therefore, whatever you may have read or learned about affirmations should be set aside if you would succeed with the instructions given in these lessons. If you have become so fond of the use of affirmations through an intimate acquaintance with them, and because of their alluring attractiveness you cannot reject all that you have read and learned about them, at least take these pretty beliefs of yours and wrap them up for the time being; place them in your treasure chest among the family heirlooms and rare possessions of this material world, until such time as you have become familiar and well acquainted with the newer ideas contained in this book. Then, after you are as intimate with these new opinions as you are with the others, you may occupy a rainy Sunday by taking the old ones from their hiding places and comparing them with the newer ones, and decide for yourself which you shall make your real jewels and your ornaments of life. But until you are as well acquainted with the use of the new tools as you are with the old ones, and until you have given the newer principles as much time to prove their efficacy and demonstrate their power as you have given the older ones in your hopes and frustrated realizations, you are not competent to judge which will serve you best, and you will not be fair to yourself in rejecting what is now offered to you.

For the Home and Business

Therefore, proceed with these new ideas with an open mind, and without bias or prejudice give them an opportunity to register their logical basis and appeal to your common sense, and you will soon find that you have contacted a new world of possibilities and a new life of realities.

CHAPTER II

THE COSMIC AND YOU

HERE are two very universal ideas connected with the practical application of psychology and metaphysics in the Occidental world which are generally associated with affirmations, and with conscious or subconscious ideas held by those who are seeking the blessings of the Cosmic.

One of the ideas is that each one of us "is at one with God," or "a child of God's perfect manifestation." The other idea is that "the abundant supply of the Cosmos is at our disposal," or "the blessings of God are mine."

With both or either one of these ideas as a fundamental belief, it is natural for a man or woman to feel that suffering and pain, disease and ill-health, poverty or the lack of necessities in life, are not only essentially wrong but due entirely to some trick of the mortal mind or some lack of realization of Divine or Cosmic contact.

If it were true that ill-health and suffering or disease were the result of some mental trick of the mortal mind, or some aberration of the mortal mind's memory of its Divine attunement, then we would be justified in believing that it would be necessary only to untrick the mind, or to establish a conscious realization of Divine attunement, in order to cleanse the body or the consciousness of all suffering, disease, and pain. In other words, if all pain and suffering were the result of some false reasoning on the part of the mind, and both the cause and the manifestation of disease and pain were the reactions of a false belief within the mortal mind alone, then it would be logical to conclude that the cleansing of the mind's conceptions and the repeated affirmation that disease and pain do not exist would alter the conditions and leave one free from all suffering.

But such is not the case, fortunately. I say fortunately, even though on the face of the matter it seems that it would be a very fortunate thing if all disease and suffering were the result of mere mistaken beliefs in the mortal mind, for that would seemingly leave healing and health easily attainable. But it is fortunate that such is not the case, for that would eventually demonstrate the superiority of the dominion of mortal mind over the will of man, or over the fundamental and natural laws of the universe; and that cannot be, for man is ever and anon subject to natural laws and spiritual laws, all of which are laws of God.

Man cannot change, regulate, or modify—least of all negate and set aside—any of the natural laws or any of the spiritual laws. He must abide by them! But he has the will, and with it the privilege and power of using natural law, and spiritual law, to regulate his life. He must abide by these laws, and he may cooperate with them or run counter to them. Nevertheless, he is ever affected by them, and his hope and salvation from disease, pain and suffering, poverty and discomfort, lie in cooperating with natural and spiritual laws and applying them to his own advancement and perfection, rather than running counter to them.

Disease and suffering, poverty and discomfort, are invariably the result of the violation of natural or spiritual laws. The sufferer, or the victim of circumstances, may not always be the one who has violated the law, for it is true that "unto the third and fourth generation will the law make itself manifest." But regardless of the cause, and regardless of who violated the laws, the sufferer therefrom and the victim thereof has it within his or her power to adjust the conditions by directing, in his or her behalf, the operation of other natural and spiritual laws, and living in harmony with them.

It is perfectly true that as human beings we are the highest expression of God's creation. It is also true that being created in His spiritual image, we are children of His Consciousness and an intimate part of His own being. Therefore, it is more than a mere logical conclusion that we are children of love, perfectly created, and having within us the creative powers and the essential goodness and Divinity of God's own Consciousness. But this alone is not sufficient to prevent the development of disease within our bodies, or to keep us continually healthy and happy, regardless of our own voluntary actions and our methods of living and thinking. Man may create a perfect piece of machinery, and if it is misused, or if it is allowed to be neglected or damaged, it will cease to be the perfect thing it was or could be.

It is useless to argue the point as to whether God also created evil and disease, suffering, pain, and poverty, as the opposites of all that is good. The fact is that such things do exist, and what we should be concerned with in any practical study of metaphysics or ontology is the cause of their existence in our own affairs, in our own environments, or within our own bodies.

Regardless of whether God created the dark night as well as the bright day, we know that the night is caused by the absence of light. And we know likewise that light will dispel darkness. We know these things because they are demonstrations of natural law, and spiritual law. And we have come to realize that to affirm in the darkness that there is no darkness, results in no effulgence of light. The mystic may have his symbolical interpretation of light and may have his metaphysical understanding of darkness, but he does not allow his symbolical light to become a material thing, nor his metaphysical darkness to become such an equivocal thing that in the midst of actual darkness he affirms the existence of light, and denies the existence of its opposite. He knows that there is but one thing that will dispel darkness, and that is light. And he knows that there is but one thing that will affirm the light, and that is the actual light itself.

So it is that a practical mystic, trained in the Rosicrucian principles, is aware of the fact that all disease and suffering have resulted from the violation of natural laws, or the failure to abide by natural laws through a voluntary disobedience of their authority.

To return to the familiar toothache, we may say that the tooth aches because of some cause within the tooth. The cause is a diseased condition of the tooth, or the gums surrounding the tooth. This diseased condition is a result of the violation of some law of nature. The violation was not a metaphysical one, a mystical one, nor a mere trick of the mortal mind in believing that it had violated some law.

It is difficult for man to imagine that which he has never experienced nor realized. The mind that has never realized the agony of a toothache cannot conceive or imagine it, and produce through its imagination a synthetic demonstration.

The mortal mind can be conscious of a toothache only through having the experience. The mortal mind may give a false eminence to the toothache, or may attribute to it a mistaken sense of authority, and it may even credit the toothache with the right to enslave its victim. But it cannot create that toothache, nor can it negate it out of existence. The ache is a pain, and the pain is the result of a cause, and mortal mind cannot create the cause nor can it remove the cause.

As we have said in the previous chapter, the Oriental mystic has used affirmations and his will power to prevent the mortal mind from giving undue power and authority to the ache or its cause to enslave him. He has learned how to negate the mortal mind's acceptance of a false belief in the power of pain to enslave him, but he has never prostituted his correct understanding of the use of such a negative affirmation to the imbecilic practice of positively affirming the non-existence of the pain itself.

The Rosicrucian, as a practical mystic, with his feet firmly on the ground during his earthly existence, and ever conscious of the material laws as well as the spiritual laws, uses his will in directing the natural creative forces within his body, and throughout the universe, to remove the *cause* of pain and to cure the toothache by curing the condition which resulted from the violation of some natural law.

As we have intimated, this is practical mysticism. It is reasonable, rational, and sound in every way. It neither denies the existence of God and His means and methods, nor does it aggrandize the material part of man and make him superior to the spiritual part of his being.

The abundant supply does exist, not only in the Cosmic, but throughout all of nature. God has provided bountifully for all the needs and most of the luxuries required or desired by every human being. These constitute the rich blessings which God promised His creatures and which He has so beautifully demonstrated throughout all the ages.

Whatever may be lacking in your life, whatever may be wanting among your needs, exists for you to possess, to have and to hold, so long as you use it rightfully. What you lack is not in your possession, or at your disposal, because you have not attuned yourself to it, or have not attracted it to yourself. Affirming that you have it when you do not have it, will not attract or manifest it. Nor will the belief that since you do not have it, you cannot have it, affect the fact that you still may have it if you earn it, deserve it, or attract it and bring it into your consciousness.

All things that man may require are his essentially and potentially, but they may not be his actually, because of some principle, some law exercised by him or denied by him which withholds the realization of the things that he lacks.

To affirm, therefore, that since we are perfectly created and perfect in the image of God, we shall have no disease, regardless of how we think, live, or act, is as inconsistent as saying that regardless of the fact that it is the middle of the night, and by natural and Divine law, the sun does not shine, the sun is still shining because we have affirmed that the sun exists and the darkness is not.

And to affirm that because there is an abundant supply for all, and essentially every blessing and bounty of God is at our disposal, we therefore have everything, and lack nothing, while at the time we are objectively conscious of our needs, is simply proclaiming a falsehood and hoping that our own predicament will be magically changed by a formula that is as unscientific and unsound metaphysically as anything can be.

Therefore, in a practical way, I shall attempt to show you how we may attract and bring into our existence the things which we lack, and which our Divine perfection and the abundant supply have established for us.

Chapter III

MENTAL ALCHEMY

O NE of the most popular beliefs in the Occidental world regarding the application of psychological principles to our everyday affairs is in connection with the so-called "art of concentration."

It is generally believed, by those who have heard the public lecturer propound the simpleness of modern psychology, that through concentration upon a specific need some magical processes are set into action, which bring into materialization the thing desired. It matters little what the thing may be, or when or how we concentrate upon it, for according to the various lecturers and teachers of this "art," there are as many methods as there are teachers who offer their personal instruction.

One public lecturer, renowned for her years of devotion to the expounding of the simple formulas of psychological magic, frankly admits that after investigating her own private formula for many years, and examining the reports of her thousands of paying students, she can guarantee her concentration method to be sixty-five per cent efficient! It would seem that if there is any psychological, metaphysical, or mystical law involved in the "art of concentration," one hundred per cent efficiency should be guaranteed as the standard. Thirty-five per cent admittedly fail, according to this one lecturer.

My own investigations, and the reports I have received from perhaps fifty thousand persons who have tried all of the personally discovered and unique systems of concentration taught in the "Fifty Dollars for Seven Lessons" assemblies conducted by these itinerant teachers, have shown that ten per cent of the tests of such methods produce results which may be attributed to the practice.

Yet it cannot be denied that there is an art in concentrating, and that this art can be used to bring into our lives the things which we desire or which we need. There is a method known to the Rosicrucians which is easily guaranteed to be one hundred per cent efficient, if used as directed, but of this I may speak later. The point I wish to make is that there is nothing wrong with the principle of concentration, but there is much wrong with the system for its use—as presented by those who foster in the minds of the public the false belief that it is a simple process, requiring no other consideration than to concentrate, wish for something, and desire to turn the wish into materialization.

It is an easily demonstrable fact that of the many things we need in our lives, or wish for the most, those things upon which we concentrate our attention and our thoughts most continuously and sincerely are likely to be brought into realization. It would be a trite thing to say that through concentration upon a desire, we tend to bring it into realization. But the fact remains that there is a considerable difference between centering our conscious thoughts upon our great desire and keeping it foremost in our consciousness, and the so-called secret methods of concentrating on each and every little thing that appears upon the prospective horizon as a necessity or a desirability.

Without doubt, we are more apt to bring into our lives that thing to which we devote most of our attention, or to which we give the utmost thought. When we become obsessed with a wish, a hope, or a desire, to such an extent that it blots out all other temptations and puts far into the background all other seeming needs or wants, we are very likely to make every one of our acts contribute toward the fulfillment or realization of the wish, and to expend every possible effort as a contributing factor in its materialization.

I have found, through conversations with hundreds of individuals who have been especially selected to discuss with me their wants—because of their importance or their seriousness in the scheme of things—that on the part of the individual there has been an entire absence of true concentration in the proper manner upon the thing desired.

Let me illustrate my point with a typical example. A young man was brought to me by his father, who was a very successful banker and general business man. The son was twenty-four years of age, and for five years had been employed in the bookkeeping and record office of one of the largest lumber companies in the West. The father had wanted the boy to start at the bottom of whatever industry or profession he chose, and had been quite satisfied with the youth's connection with the lumber company when he first secured the position. But both the son and the father were now restless because there seemed to be no special opportunity for advancement with the lumber concern, and the boy did not care to go into the banking business, or into any other business, in fact, but had what he called "a great hope." He hoped to become a good architect, with a big practice, and with the opportunity to create wonderful buildings and beautiful homes.

The father agreed that the boy's ambition was noble, and had offered to pay the boy's way through one of the universities if he wished to take the complete course in architecture. But the boy had refused the offer, insisting that he would not have his education paid for nor accept any further money from his father, but would work his way through life. I believe that secretly this proud attitude on the part of the boy pleased the father, but the problem was this: How was the boy to become an architect?

The boy admitted that he had held this desire and wish to become an architect for many years.

He said it was his dream, and his hope. He had always heard that if one held fast to a belief, a hope, or an ambition, or had maintained that wish steadfastly for a number of years, that it would lead the person on some path toward the goal desired. Yet here he was, doing the same work in the same way, day after day, with no indication that his great dream was to be fulfilled.

I asked the boy if he had concentrated upon this great hope or dream, and he enthusiastically replied that it was the only thing he concentrated upon day and night. He had no other particular ambition, he said, and had laid aside all social desires as dependent upon his success in attaining his great hope.

Careful questioning revealed that his idea of concentration was much like that of the tramp who sits upon the park bench and looks across the lawns toward the home of the wealthy man, and wishes that he could be inside at the dining table to enjoy the excellent meal and the comfort of the fireplace, and he wishes and wishes and wishes. Unquestionably every time the tramp is hungry he wishes he had a meal, and every time he sees others in comfort and luxury while he is cold and uncomfortable he wishes he had the pleasures of life which others enjoy. These wishes of his receive considerable concentration at those times when he is most impressed with his poverty and discomfort. But can one say that such intermittent wishing, or the holding of one consistent desire, constitutes the art of concentrating?

The young man referred to above admitted that in the lumber company's office where he worked, he met, almost daily, the architects who came there to secure important data or to discuss their plans with the executives of the company. He was constantly brought into intimate contact with builders and contractors, and he met a great many persons who discussed in his presence the intricate problems of architecture and building. Careful questioning revealed that he had not concentrated enough on his great dream to have made the dream an obsessional desire. The dream had not become so dominating a factor in all of his thinking and acting as to have led him into conversation with architects as to how he might advance himself from his present position, to that of a student of architecture, without going to college. He had not even been tempted by his hope or his dream to visit architects at their homes, or their offices, and watch them at work. He had not been urged by his dream or his hope to borrow any of their books, or preliminary guides to the art of architecture. He had not even expressed his dream or his hope to anyone except his parents and one or two friends. Even his employer did not know that he was anxious to become an architect, nor did the draftsmen of the lumber concern have even a suspicion that this young man was anxious to take up the study of architecture, and thereby become a valuable aid to the concern for which he was working. Concentration, indeed!

There is a considerable difference between concentrating upon a dream or a hope, and concentrating upon the fulfillment thereof.

Had this young man been truly concentrating on bringing his dream into realization, he would have talked architecture, thought architecture, and acted architecture every moment of his life. He could not have been kept away from the presence of architects, nor away from the drawing boards, bookshelves of architects' offices, and from draftsmen's rooms. Real concentration on his great hope would have led him within a year to trying his hand at making plans and drawings, and undoubtedly he would have fallen in with those who would have advised him and helped him, even while holding his position and earning an income. And his employer declared later that he would have gladly admitted him to work in the drafting room in his spare hours, to learn some of the practical lessons of the first stages of creative building.

Let us take another example. A young man, nineteen years of age, working in a photographic studio doing the commonplace work at the average wages, had occasion to see some special work brought to the studio to be copied, and its very nature, beauty, and rareness attracted his attention. He found that the pictures brought into the studio to be copied were the result of a little-known process, almost secretly used by a few men in New York City who had learned the art in foreign lands and were capable, not only of making the most attractive and beautiful reproductions of nature ever exhibited in art galleries, but of earning an unusual income, enabling them to live well and enjoy many of the luxuries of life. The young man became obsessed with the desire to learn this unusual art, and devote himself to it. The idea—the hope—the ambition—came into birth almost spontaneously as he listened to his employer's story of the rareness, beauty, and profits connected with this fascinating art. For many days, the young man dreamed about it, and gradually his ambition became an all-absorbing, dominating obsession of his consciousness.

In every spare moment he visited art galleries and art stores, seeking to view other specimens of this art. He soon learned that the art was rare enough and the specimens few and in great demand. While walking or riding through the parks or busy streets, his eye was ever alert to the beauties of nature which might be reproduced by this unique process. In every magazine and newspaper he saw pictures or read of incidents that would be worthy of reproduction if he could use the secret process. During the evening he spent every possible moment in libraries, searching for any possible clue that might lead him to some description of the secret methods. He talked about it, he dreamed about it, he lived his hope. Every conscious moment was centered upon doing those things, learning those things, thinking those thoughts, and arranging those thoughts which would bring him nearer to his ambition. He was concentrating in the true sense of the word upon what he wanted, and there was no mystical, secret principle about his concentration so far as he knew.

He was unaware of any psychological principles involved in his devotion to the one dream of his life. He did not go to fortune tellers, crystal gazers, palm readers, or card prophets to find whether he would ever succeed in materializing his dream. He had no question in his mind, no doubt in his consciousness that he had selected the mission of his life, and that it would be realized. Finally his great urge and concentration led him to locate the man who had brought the first specimens to the studio. He found reason to call on him in a business way with other matters connected with the art, during the hours when the man would be working at his process. In hurried interviews with the man, his eyes registered everything within sight, with that keenness that comes through real concentration. He saw labels on bottles, names on instruments, imprints on catalogues, in the man's workroom. He hurried to stores, and to factories, and purchased similar instruments, chemicals, and other things, little by little as his means afforded. He experimented by following the very brief and almost enigmatic instructions that accompanied each thing he bought, and finally, through meditation, concentration, and inspiration, there seemed to come to him shafts of light in the form of bits of wisdom that informed him, as if intuitively, how to experiment, and what to do. The results were small, crude specimens of pictures which were far from being admirable, but were, nevertheless, unique in their process. Finally he took several of these to the man who knew the whole art, and the man was so astounded at the youth's "discovery" of part of the secret formula, or process, of this hidden art that he unintentionally perhaps, or diplomatically, told the young man where he had made some errors, and why his work was not what it should be. This led to further experiments which produced better results, and within a few months the young man had evolved a process of his own which produced pictures equal to those of the eminent artist whose work had inspired him. Within a year his success in this effort was bringing him an income and a recognition in the art world, never equalled by any youth in the past, and within another year, his dream and hope were being fulfilled abundantly.

Concentration did it! But it was not the form of concentration that is taught in "Five Lessons for Five Dollars," nor learned in a dollar book on "how to concentrate upon the abundant supply for your needs."

The Rosicrucians know that truly to concentrate means to have one absorbing idea at a time, and to think of it to the exclusion of everything else, and then let your entire life, for the time being, cooperate with your concentration to bring into realization the thing that you desire.

This does not mean that to concentrate successfully the dreamer, or the thinker, must take himself away from his profession, his business, his duty, or his obligations, and isolate himself in a cave or on a mountaintop where he can do nothing else but think and meditate upon his one desire. That would surely frustrate every possibility of fulfillment. Nor does it mean that concentration should be indulged in only when the mind is free and the body is at rest before the fireside in the evening, or upon retiring at night. It means concentration in every possible moment of relaxation from the duties at hand. It means sacrificing every other thought that is not productive or essential. It means devoting every spare moment and every moment that is not absolutely necessary to life and its duties. It means forsaking the pleasures and temptations, and the casual things of life, for more profound and more extended thought upon the one desire. It means time, for it requires time. It means effort, for it requires mental activity, not passivity. It means action, for it cannot be associated with relaxation and dormancy of the faculties. It requires faith and confidence, for the elements of doubt and suspicion will frustrate every possibility of fulfillment.

As we proceed with these little talks in the next chapters, the art of proper concentration will be made plain and more practical.

One of the most important principles, however, which must be understood and brought into use before concentration becomes useful, is that of mental alchemy. The Rosicrucians of the past were well known as pre-eminent alchemists. Not only have they been credited with having succeeded in making pure gold out of dross metals, and thereby bringing into realization one of their fond dreams, but it has been conceded that the Rosicrucian art, with its unusual teachings and knowledge, enables its students and adepts alchemically to bring into materialization everything that they can mentally conceive and create in imagination.

Thus they were proficient in the art of mental alchemy as well as in the alchemy of the crucible and physical alchemy.

Man alone, of all creatures, has within his being creative powers which are a part of the God Consciousness; thus man is uniquely endowed. He has the rare privilege and ability to concentrate and create mentally that which he desires to create eventually in material form. In this process of mentally conceiving and mentally creating, man is the equal in some degree of God Himself, since it is a God-given privilege for man to use the creative power which brought into existence in this universe all that is.

But the art of mentally creating is little understood in the Occidental world, and is practiced almost exclusively by those adepts who are often considered to be the white magicians of this earth.

I say they are considered "the white magicians" for their magic is white magic, free from evil, and free from any destructive nature, for the power which they use is part of the creative power of the God Consciousness, and this creative power is incapable of creating that which is evil, or that which is destructive.

The undeveloped or unevolved mind of man may conceive of evil and of things destructive, but man cannot mentally create or bring them into materialization in the mystical manner by which good and constructive things will come into material form when created by the Cosmic power in the mind.

When man conceives of that which is not good, and seeks to bring it from his mind into material form, he must labor with the grossly material elements and bring them into irrational, illogical, and unnatural relationship, in order to make them manifest as evil in the material realm. But when man conceives of that which is good, and constructive, he may mentally create it by the alchemical processes of his mind, in attunement with the alchemical processes of the Cosmos, and as a result of such attunement the thing he created will sooner or later become manifest outwardly through the creative processes existing within his consciousness and his being.

It is, therefore, only necessary for one who seeks an improvement in environment, an answer to his needs, or a beneficent item added to his possessions, mentally to create the thing he desires through concentration and mental visualization. He should do this day by day, hour by hour, whenever the time permits, until the thing conceived of and in the process of creation, becomes a living, vital, vibrating thing in his own consciousness. It must become so real that its reality is omnipresent, and so effectual in its existence that it modifies, controls, directs, and influences his thinking, his acting, and his living.

Such a mental creation soon ceases to appear to be a thing of the mind alone. When the eyes are closed, it is clearly seen; when the mind is in relaxation it takes possession of his being. It is ever present in all of its forms, color, size, weight, and power, regardless of its nature. It is like the unborn in the womb of its parent, ready for delivery into this material world.

All things which God created were first conceived by God in this manner. All things which materialize on this earth as blessings for man and contributions to his essential needs were alchemically created in the Cosmic before their existence was projected into material form on this earth plane. Man must therefore exemplify and emulate the Cosmic processes and the Divine scheme. He cannot materialize into this world that which he has conceived without the proper process of maturing development.

In my experience with business men, firms, boards of directors, and corporations which have labored incorrectly and therefore unsuccessfully with great plans or important matters, I have found that that which they desired to bring about had not been properly conceived in the first place. Seeds which are lacking in consistent relationship, or which are unimportant in nature, inharmonious in vibration, or the offspring of evil parents, cannot be brought together to effect a perfect conception or to vitalize an idea. And I have found that even where the conception was complete and more or less perfect in every requisite, there had been no period for proper gestation, and no logical, natural course of development to bring the conception into a living, vibrant form for final expression.

It is fortunate, indeed, for man that all his passing conceptions, and that all of his mental images do not take form and parade about him to enslave his being and clutter the world with the hermaphrodites of misconception. It is fortunate that only those things can come into being, into concrete and material realization, which have been carefully synthesized and developed in the crucible of the mental laboratory of man's Divine consciousness. But because there is this element of time, and this necessity for proper development and maturity, man becomes impatient and seeks shorter methods and easier ways to bring his dreams and his desires into fulfillment. In this he most surely fails, and through such failure loses faith and confidence and dethrones the creative power within him as a pretender.

It is not a difficult thing for the human mind to visualize in all of its details that which the mind can conceive as a thing desired. It must be done through the concentration of the objective faculties, and the use of the will power directed from the outer self inwardly, as though there were within the human consciousness a sanctum for the preparation and creation of all things desired by man.

Little by little, part by part, element by element, the thing must be put together in its visualized form, and after each addition of each stage of development, it must be examined, tested, and tried, to discover if any element has been overlooked, any part neglected, or any adjustment or association of parts and elements wrongly made. As one would build a house by constructing the walls, brick by brick, so each part of the thing desired must be mentally created and visualized, until it is ready to burst forth in its completed state and stand in the consciousness of the creator as a thing actually existing and in his possession.

So much for mental alchemy—the art of mentally creating and visualizing the thing desired. Nothing pertaining to the desire must be overlooked. One must keep in mind the usefulness of the thing desired. One must avoid attempting to create that which has no practical use and which will bring neither profit nor benefit to anyone. The dangers from its misuse must be considered and provided against during the process of creating. Its benefits to others must be included, and it must be so created that it cannot fail to be useful to others, and to be of benefit generally to humanity. It must be so created or of such a nature that when it comes into final manifestation objectively, it will become no charge upon the happiness, peace, health, and contentment of others, nor carry with it the sacrifices and sorrow of others. It must be desired with as little selfishness as is consistent with the need of the thing. Its possession must be inspired by no motive associated with revenge or anger, hatred or jealousy, pride or arrogance. Its development and growing reality in the consciousness of its creator should occasionally inculcate a sense of humility and humbleness, for as it comes into form, the magnificence of the creative powers of man should make the creator of each thing realize his obligation to God and his attunement with God's kingdom.

If all of these things are considered, and made a part of the process, then truly one may feel that success and satisfying realization are imminent and assured.

CHAPTER IV

COMMANDING COSMIC HELP

HE real mystic knows that he must work through the Cosmic and with Cosmic law in order to bring about the realization of his conceived and visualized dreams and plans. He never forgets the Cosmic law, and he never fails to take the Cosmic into partnership in all his plans and desires.

But there is a great difference between *commanding* Cosmic help and *demanding* Cosmic help. One may command Cosmic help through one's worthiness, sincerity, loyalty, and devotion to Cosmic ideals, but one can never demand anything from the Cosmic, for the attitude of demanding would immediately preclude any consideration on the part of the Cosmic for the wishes and desires of the petitioner.

Still, we read in many popular forms of applied psychology, and even in much of the so-called mystical literature of the day, how one may demand of the Cosmic or through the Cosmic, the realization, mediate and immediate, of those things greatly desired. Such an idea is responsible for the many failures that thousands have had in trying to bring about concrete demonstrations of mystical processes.

Before giving you the definite methods for bringing about certain hopes and ambitions in your life, I wish to complete these preliminary lessons by devoting the next few pages to a proper explanation of how you may secure the cooperation of the Cosmic, and how you may avoid interfering with the Cosmic methods for cooperation.

When one seeks the cooperation of the Cosmic in bringing about a realization of some plan, one assumes that the Cosmic can help, and while it knows how to help, and is unlimited in its means and methods, it would be almost futile to ask the Cosmic to help in many of the problems which man has to solve. It is natural to think that no man or woman will appeal to the Cosmic for help in regard to a proposition or plan which can be easily worked out by the man or woman, independently of the Cosmic. Surely we do not appeal to the Cosmic for help every moment of the day in mastering the minor routine things of life. We have learned what our own possibilities as individuals are, because of the Cosmic creative powers resident within us, and that most of our daily tasks and passing problems are solved or mastered without appeal to the Cosmic. This is precisely as it should be, and as God and the Cosmic intended it to be. We appeal to the Cosmic only when our plans seem to meet insurmountable obstacles, or when our efforts and endeavors have been frustrated, and the efforts and endeavors of others around us seem to be of no avail. The mystic knows that he should *not* bring to the Cosmic—which is the court of last appeal in a mystical sense—any problem which can be solved without its help.

We must not forget the ancient injunction that by the sweat of our brows shall we labor and produce the necessary things of life. He who labors diligently and persistently in an effort to produce and bring about the things he needs in life, meets with the greatest success, while he who dreams and plans and expects the Cosmic to labor for him in the fulfillment of the thing he dreams, is doomed to failure. Yet that is precisely the situation in this country today as a result of the mistaken information that has been taught and disseminated by so-called practical psychologists and new thought teachers.

As stated above, Cosmic help can be secured and should be secured at such times as the individual is incapable of coping with the situation, or the situation is one which is beyond human control, or of such a general nature or intense nature that too many problems or points are involved for one mind to master.

Assuming, therefore, that the Cosmic can help through unlimited means and methods at its disposal, we must realize at once that any attempt to tell the Cosmic *how* to bring about the desires or plans uppermost in our minds, is not only an imposition on the intelligence and universal wisdom of the Cosmic, but it is one of the most frequent and positive reasons for the negative results that are so universally attained.

Let me state this point again, in another way, so as to give it the utmost emphasis. Since the Cosmic has unlimited ways and means of carrying out anything that it decides to do, wishes to do, or agrees to do, it is inconsistent and injurious to the success of the plans to tell the Cosmic how to work out the solution. However, this is precisely what thousands are doing in every attempt they make to secure Cosmic cooperation, and I hope that this particular lesson from me will prevent anyone from ever forgetting the fundamental principles explained at this time.

Now let me take an example of the wrong method, and see if you can grasp the point in a manner that will register definitely on your mind for a long time. Let us assume that a man has a piece of property which he is anxious to release. He does not wish to carry the taxes and insurance any longer, and prefers to have the cash so that he may use it right away to buy railroad tickets for himself and family, and start for the West. Here he wishes to establish his home and secure a new position in order to start life over again under better conditions and in a better part of the country. He has tried every known method to sell his piece of property. He has tried real estate agents, real estate brokers, newspaper advertising, and personal solicitation. After many months, he has lined up a few prospective buyers, but after all this time the total result of his efforts consists merely of a prospective sale to one of three persons.

One of these persons would pay him the money immediately if he could get his case settled in court, which would bring him enough money to buy the property, but the case is in the hands of a referee who delays in rendering his decision. Prospect number two would buy the property immediately, except for the fact that his business is in the hands of a receiver and he is waiting for cash to come as a result of a settlement among creditors and others. Prospect number three is a young man who wants to buy the property to begin the life of farming, but his father is in Europe, and will not return for several months, and the son is waiting for the father to send him money by mail or cable, but does not seem to be able to get it.

Now then, our man who wants to sell the property and go West to live feels that he should appeal to the Cosmic for help. He proceeds to concentrate on the Cosmic and to visualize what he would like to have made manifest. He follows the typical system outlined in modern psychology courses, and so he sits down and projects to the Cosmic mind his requests and demands, about as follows: He says to the Cosmic, "Now I want to sell my property, so that I can go West and buy a home and start life over again, and I cannot sell my property unless one of these three prospects secures his money. Therefore, please help the man to have the referee make a favorable decision, or the receiver to bring about a settlement of that man's business, or the father in Europe to send money to his son." Then, our concentrating friend proceeds to concentrate upon and visualize the referee working over the legal papers and reaching a decision to release the money that the one prospect needs. Then he visualizes the receiver working over his papers and coming to a favorable decision for prospect number two. Then he visualizes the father in Europe reading the boy's letters and deciding to send the boy the money.

After doing all this, and spending half an hour in concentration and visualization, he feels quite sure that he has made perfectly plain to the Cosmic just what he wants. And he waits day after day for the Cosmic to manifest its solution and no manifestation occurs. Naturally he wishes to know what is wrong.

Now let us look at this man's problem and see whether or not he has been doing the right thing. In the first place, when this man consulted me—and I have selected this case from an actual occurrence—he impressed upon me very strongly the fact that his great desire was to sell his piece of property to one of these three prospects so that he could get the money and start for the West.

That was the uppermost thought in his mind in all of his concentrations, and in all of his appeals to the Cosmic. And yet I am sure that each one of you will agree with me right now when I say to you that after all is said and done, what the man wanted least of all was to sell his property and get the money. In fact, the sale of his property and the securing of money was not the vital issue or the real thing that he desired most. What the man really wanted was to get out into the West and start life over again. I convinced him of this by saying to him, "Suppose you did not sell your property, but had an offer from a firm in California to come out to that state and manage one of its big factories, and this offer was accompanied by a promise to pay all your traveling expenses, and aid you in locating a nice home. Would you accept that offer?" He immediately replied, "That is the very thing I want, and I would gladly accept the offer."

So you see, the real desire of this man's dreams or hopes was not to sell the piece of property. From his limited, material, earthly viewpoint, there was only one way by which he could get out West and start life over again, and that was by selling his property and using the money to carry out his plans. He never, for one moment, thought of the possibility that the Cosmic might have other ways of bringing about a fulfillment of his desires. In other words, his desire was to get out West; and he had sat down and reasoned it out, and figured it out from his point of view and had decided arbitrarily and finally, that there was only one way for him to master his problems, which was by selling his property. Then he proceeded in all the rest of his thinking, planning, and concentrating, to use his arbitrary decision, his final conclusion, his reason and judgment, as being the ultimate, the perfect, the only way to bring about a realization. Having once decided this way, he proceeded then to tell the Cosmic that it should or must accept his decision, his plan, his solution, and work it out for him. Certainly that is an imposition upon the Cosmic, and at the same time it was the worst thing he could do to bring about the realization he expected.

In other words, the man was appealing to the Cosmic to sell his property, instead of appealing to the Cosmic to help him to get out West and start a new life. Or, in another way, we may say that he was saying to the Cosmic, "I want your help in bringing about a realization of my plans; but listen, Cosmic, I have decided how it should be done and how it can come about, and how you should assist. I am going to tell you just what I want you to do, and I want my plans fulfilled in just this way and no other. I do not want you to drop any money out of the sky into my lap. I do not want you to have any money come to me through a will or through a gift, or through any other channel, but through the sale of my property. I do not want you to send me railroad tickets through some firm that would like to have me come West. I do not want you to give me the railroad tickets through some banking institution that would help me to go out West. I do not want you to have a representative of a Western company call on me and offer to pay my expenses, but I want you to give me the money solely through the sale of my property. I do not want you to have any company offer me a position or a home in the West. I want to go there with my family, and hunt a position, find one in my own way, and bring about that end of the plan through my own efforts. I do not want you to do anything unique or original that I have not thought of, but simply follow out my instructions and then I will know that the Cosmic is my partner."

Now I will leave it to the common sense of my reader as to whether or not such reasoning and such appealing to the Cosmic is apt to bring the desired results or not. The proof of my contention lies in the fact that after I had talked to this man and pointed out the limitations that he was putting around the solution of his problem, and the dictatorial attitude he had taken toward the Cosmic, he went home and proceeded to concentrate in the proper manner, and succeeded in having his hopes fulfilled abundantly. He concentrated on the following picture: He saw himself and wife traveling, not particularly by train or by automobile or in any definite form, to the West. He pictured himself meeting a group of men who offered him a good position. He saw his wife and himself entering into a cozy home, without attempting to visualize that home with a porch or without a porch, two stories high, or one story high, painted red or painted green, with big yards or little yards, but just a home, comfortable and in accordance with what he actually needed. This is all that he had in mind when he concentrated, and appealed to the Cosmic. He was absolutely indifferent as to whether he bought the tickets or someone else bought the tickets; whether he went this week or next week; or what part of the State of California he reached or what kind of position it was that was offered to him. All of these minor details and ways and means he left entirely to the Cosmic.

What was the result? One of his friends who had casually written to an acquaintance in the

West about this man's desires, received a letter stating that there was an opening in a new shoe factory to be established in the West, and since this man had been a former superintendent of a shoe factory, there was a possibility of a position for him. This letter from the West was shown to the man who was concentrating, and he wrote direct to the new factory in California and was offered the position, plus an advancement of his salary sufficient to bring him and his family to the West.

In twelve days he was on the train westward bound. Precisely three weeks after he had reached the West and was settled in his new home and new position, a real estate firm in New York notified him that a large corporation heretofore unconsidered as a prospect for the buying of the property had made a very good offer for his property, and that the offer had come "out of the blue." Hence our man found himself comfortably and happily settled in a new home, in a new position, and in a new part of the country, plus a nice sum of money which he could put away in a savings bank and hold for a rainy day. All of his dreams and hopes had been fulfilled, and even more, and yet not one detail of the realization was similar to what he had been concentrating upon in his original attempts to demand of the Cosmic its cooperation.

In another illustration: A widow sought a definite means to earn an income in order to support her fourteen-year-old son so that he might continue at school, go on through high school, and prepare himself to support his mother and keep up the home. Before appealing to the Cosmic for help, she also reasoned as to the proper way of bringing about her hopes, and she decided after talking with a number of other women, that there was only one thing she could do to earn an income, and that was to make paper flowers and have her son either peddle them or deliver them to some stores or novelty shops in various parts of the city where she lived. She had reached this conclusion by analyzing herself and determining, as she explained to me, that since she had no business training, knew nothing of stenography or typing, and was not an artist or a musician, there was no other way for her to earn an income.

In other words, after fifteen or twenty minutes'

self-analysis, she was fully convinced that she knew all about herself, knew all she could possibly do in this world to contribute to its needs or to produce anything of usefulness. I may say, in passing, that this is one of the big mistakes a great many persons make in connection with their personal problems. They attempt to decide what possibilities they have in this world. They believe themselves to be the best judges, even better than the Cosmic or God Himself. And whatever conclusion they may reach regarding their capabilities and limitations is always ultimate, final, supreme, and quite definite. It never dawns upon the minds of these persons that there may be a higher and better judge, or that there may be an intelligence that knows better than any living being just what they can do in life. It never seems to come to the minds of these persons that each one of us has a certain mission to fulfill in life, that in order to fulfill this mission there are various means by which it may be brought about, and that God or the Cosmic may know more about this than we do.

However, the widow referred to proceeded to concentrate day after day for several weeks, asking the Cosmic to help her boy dispose of these paper flowers, which were very inferior in quality and unattractive in finish because of her inexperience. The poor boy was neglecting his studies and tiring out his young body trying to sell these flowers from place to place. He had very little success, and as the family funds became exhausted, and the cold weather threatened many days of suffering and privation, the widow came to me in desperation and explained her problem. She wanted to know how to get the Cosmic to help her sell flowers! All she could think of was the sale of flowers, and the continuance of her efforts to make and dispose of them.

When I asked her why she wanted to sell flowers, she said it was because she wanted to earn an income. When I asked her why she wanted to earn an income, she said it was so she could maintain her home and let the boy go to school. When I asked her why she wanted to maintain a home and let the boy go to school, she said it was because she wanted him to complete his education and be able to go into business and then support her. So we see that after all her real problem was not that of selling flowers, but of keeping her boy at school and maintaining a home. But that was not the picture she had presented to the Cosmic. That was not the picture she had concentrated upon. She had been asking the Cosmic to help bring about the ultimate desires of her heart, but at the same time she had been telling the Cosmic that it could be done only through selling flowers. Since the Cosmic probably did not agree with that plan or that decision, it did not cooperate. It had ways and means of its own of bringing about her desires, but since the widow had limited the Cosmic's cooperation to the method of selling flowers, the Cosmic offered no other form of help.

After explaining to this good women how to concentrate upon the real desire of her heart, and how to refrain from thinking about the method the Cosmic should use in working out her problem, it was brought to a manifestation in one week, and this is what happened. Another family living in a very fine home, a half mile away from her, engaged her as housekeeper with the understanding that the boy could live in the home as companion to another boy, the only child that lived in the big house. The son continued at school, and the widow continued to live more comfortably, freer from worries, and doing more constructive work for the two boys, and the couple who had engaged her, than she could have done for anyone through the making of paper flowers. The solution of her problem was one that she had never conceived of, and one which had never been suggested to her.

These two illustrations should make plain to you what I mean by concentrating on the ultimate desire of your dreams, the eventual hope in your plans, without limiting the Cosmic to ways and means of bringing it about.

In all of the explanations of methods for seeking Cosmic help, given in the following pages, it should be kept in mind that the fundamental principle outlined in this lesson should be carefully followed.

Chapter V

SECURING MONEY

NE of the two most often desired gifts from the Cosmic is, perhaps, that of money—actual cash. The other is health.

It is strange indeed that in the ultimate analysis of most of the cases where petitioners are asking the Cosmic for money we discover that it is not the actual cash in dollars and cents, or gold or silver that is desired, but the credit. There is a considerable difference between securing credit in order to enable one to purchase, buy, or secure certain necessities, and the possession of the actual cash in material form for the same purpose. And from the Cosmic point of view also, there is a considerable difference.

We would hardly think that anyone believes that the Cosmic conducts a bank and has in its vaults gold and silver, copper and nickel, as well as paper, in the form of coins and bills of all denominations, and of all countries. It would seem that only the child mind would conceive of the Cosmic being able to deposit actual money into the hands of a petitioner, like hailstones from the sky. The moment we realize that the Cosmic cannot deliver actual cash into our possession, but must bring this about through various earthly channels, we see at once that it may be that the Cosmic can aid us in our financial needs in a manner quite distinct from delivering the material form of coin to us.

Those who have read the preceding chapter will realize that in a great many cases those who are seeking or asking for money through any occult, mystical, or psychological process may not be asking for what they really need at all. I may decide that I need a new hat, and decide at the same time that I will buy it at a certain store for a certain price. In order to do this I must have the actual cash in my hand. Therefore, I proceed to concentrate upon the Cosmic to give me five dollars, seven dollars, or ten dollars, according to the price of the hat. My whole concentration is upon the amount of money that I believe I need. The purchase of the hat or the necessity for having the hat is a secondary consideration. If I proceeded properly, the hat would be the primary consideration, and whether I purchased it with actual cash, secured it on credit, or had it donated to me by a friend would be immaterial. I would be glad to leave the arrangements to the Cosmic, feeling quite satisfied if the Cosmic saw to it that I got the hat—all this provided, of course, that I was unable to earn the money and secure the hat by the sweat of the brow, as the Cosmic and all natural law intended I should.

However, there are instances where the necessity for money in some form, or for credit to an equivalent amount, is the paramount desire, and these occasions require as much serious consideration on the part of the mystic as any other necessity or desire of a legitimate nature.

From the Cosmic point of view, the use of money as it is used today is fundamentally wrong, and is a method or means arbitrarily established by man for the purpose of getting around and avoiding most of the ethical principles established by the Cosmic. I will touch on this subject in another part of these lessons, but it should be kept in mind that the Cosmic generally is not in sympathy with the use of money, and whenever and wherever it can bring about the desired results without recourse to the use of money, it will do so. Therefore, we will presume that the petitioner who is seeking for money with the help of the Cosmic will have reached the conclusion that he must have money only after analyzing his necessities very carefully, and knowing positively that nothing else but money in some form, or the equivalent credit, will serve his purpose.

Now there are two ways by which the average petitioner expects the Cosmic to help him receive his money. The first way is in asking the Cosmic to help him borrow what he needs from someone who he believes is financially capable of lending him the amount; the other way is in asking the Cosmic to help him collect either an amount that is justly coming to him, or which he expects through the settlement of some estate, will, legal paper, or other form of benevolence.

We must take each of these by itself, and consider the proper methods whereby mental or mystical laws can be used to help bring about the desired results.

For the Home and Business

When money is owed to you, and you cannot collect it because of the indifference or the temporary inability or stubbornness on the part of the person who should pay it, then you may rightfully and ethically ask the Cosmic to help you secure what is justly yours. I must warn you, however, that if there is even a fair reason for the debtor to hold back the payment while some investigation is made, or while an adjustment is made, or until you comply with some just conditions, then you cannot expect that the Cosmic is going to aid you by setting aside the rights and interests of the person who owes you the money, and force that person to make an immediate settlement with you against his own best interests. It has been found in many cases that where Mr. Jones owed a bill of one thousand dollars to Mr. Smith, and Mr. Smith was asking the Cosmic to force Mr. Jones to pay the money right away, that Mr. Jones was holding up the payment of the thousand dollars because Mr. Smith had not fully complied with the conditions that brought about the thousand-dollar obligation. It might also have been that Mr. Smith was not willing to concede some point, or to agree to some just and proper point previously arranged, or that Mr. Smith was perhaps attempting to secure the money in a shorter period than had been agreed upon. In such cases, the Cosmic will not act differently than the judge in any court would act if he knew both sides of the case.

The Cosmic will insist upon being fair to everyone, and it is simply impossible for any petitioner to come to the Cosmic with his requests and desires, thinking that he can hold back some facts about the matter and fool the Cosmic into granting him his special wishes immediately, and without investigation. If you will stop a moment you will realize that the Cosmic, if it has any mystical, universal mind and power at all, is just as familiar with the reasons, demands, and rights of the person who owes the money, as with the person who desires the money. So we have found that the petitioner seeking the payment of money which he claims is owing to him, must come to the Cosmic as he must come to a court of law, with "clean hands."

But if the money is justly due you, and there is no reason for its non-payment except the indifference or stubbornness or forgetfulness of the person who can and should pay it, then you may concentrate upon the Cosmic and, with patience, petition the Cosmic to intercede for you and see that your just debt is paid.

As to what method to use in concentrating for such a purpose, I will have more to say in a few minutes.

In asking the Cosmic to bring money to you that you believe is coming to you, or should come to you through an estate, a court settlement, a will, a legacy, or a donation of some kind, we find that here again the petitioner must be sure that he is justified in assuming and believing that the money is to be given to him and will be given to him by the giver's own volition, but that the whole affair has been delayed through forgetfulness, indecision, or something of that kind. Now we will see in this latter case, an analogy with the former case. The petitioner must again come into court with "clean hands." He must be receptive, and ready to receive the money that he desires.

It must be free from entanglements that are un-ethical, and it must not be money that will bring pleasure to the petitioner alone, and bring sorrow, suffering, and regrets to others; for in such a case the Cosmic will not think of giving its aid to the carrying out of a wish or a gift or a help of any kind that will make just one or two happy, while it makes many others sad and unhappy.

Of course there are those cases where people petition the Cosmic for some money to meet an emergency, when they have no definite idea where the money may come from, because no one owes them any particular amount, and they do not ex-pect any money through a legacy or a donation of any kind. Such a situation is a very difficult one in which to give advice and suggestions of any kind. In a great many cases of this kind, the per-son soliciting the money is not warranted in ex-pecting any from any source, and certainly is not warranted in asking the Cosmic to create an imme-diate situation wherein the petitioner is suddenly made the beneficiary of Cosmic gifts which have not been earned, arranged, or donated in any way.

Speaking in a general sense, the securing of money through Cosmic aid reduces itself to a form of concentration that is simple and effective. After having determined that the actual money is what is needed, and not the things which are to be purchased with it, then the petitioner should decide what is the precise amount, or the smallest possible amount which will meet the conditions. Not too much, or not more than is necessary, should be asked for. On the other hand, sufficient should be included in the asking to take care of the immediate, as well as the mediate, needs. This amount of money should be visualized in its figures, and not in its form.

In other words, the money should not be visualized as gold or silver, or bills, or in any particular denomination or form of currency. If one thousand dollars is desired, the figure or amount of one thousand dollars should be concentrated upon, regardless of whether that one thousand dollars will eventually show itself in the form of a check, a draft, a money order, actual cash, or a Liberty bond. And every morning, every noon, and every night, at a time just preceding the meal, the person desiring the money should attune himself through relaxation and concentration with the Cosmic and Universal Mind, and hold in his mind, at the same time, the thought and impression of the amount of money that he or she needs. After doing this for a few minutes, with the eyes either open or closed, the person should dismiss the matter by the simple statement of "This I ask of the Cosmic!" Then go about the business of the day, unconcerned about the coming of the money or the method by which the Cosmic will answer the petition.

Doing this for four or five days will unquestionably bring some result in the process leading to the realization of the amount of money desired. In addition, if this amount of money is justly owed to you by some one person, you should concentrate on that person in connection with the thousand dollars, and hold the picture of that person in your mind, along with the amount of money, so that the Cosmic will get direct from you an impression of the person who should pay the money to you. Again I must warn you about the necessity of being sure that the money is justly owed you at the moment, and that the delay in receiving it is not a just delay, and also that you are entitled to its immediate payment without further delay. Of course, after what I have said in the preceding chapter, you will not attempt to visualize how the Cosmic will make the person pay you, or just what hour it shall be handed to you, or brought to you, or placed to your credit, or otherwise made available. Such concentration upon the amount of money, and the person who owes it, three times a day for a number of days, will undoubtedly help to bring about an attitude on the part of the person who owes the money leading to action and eventual realization of your desires.

In the case where money is desired from an estate or from some person who is settling an estate, and where there is a delay or a hesitancy, or a possible frustration through so-called legal "red tape," you must be sure that there is no just reason for the delay, and that you are fully entitled to have the Cosmic come to your rescue and make immediate settlement. If you are sure of this point, then you may again visualize the amount of money desired, and with that visualization, keep in mind the person or the condition surrounding the delay, with the idea that the Cosmic will contact the right person or persons and set into action the process which will lead to the proper settlement.

It has been found that in these cases where a referee or a judge, or any other individual is attempting to make up his mind and decide whether to do a thing or not to do a thing, or whether to grant a request to one person or to another, that if the Cosmic is appealed to to bring about a decision favorable to the petitioner, the Cosmic does affect the hesitating mind of the referee, judge, or other person, and causes him suddenly to make a decision in favor of the person who is concentrating on the Cosmic for cooperation. I have known personally, of many cases where judgments or decisions have been held up for months, and in some cases years, because a certain person could not come to a definite decision and was hesitating until a proper decision could be reached. A few days' concentration, however, upon this person and upon the necessity for immediate decision, has caused the person suddenly to come to a conclusion that he has delayed too long, and now must render a favorable decision to one of the parties concerned. In several cases, an investigation afterwards or an interview with the one who made the decision, revealed that during one of the evening hours, while in relaxation, he suddenly had an impression that he must come to a certain conclusion that appeared to him to be absolutely fair and just.

You can rest assured that when the Cosmic takes up your case and impresses someone who has the right to decide with the necessity of making a decision in your favor, it is because the Cosmic knows that such a decision is just and correct. In other words, the Cosmic will not make a judge or referee or anyone else decide in your favor just because you petitioned the Cosmic to do so, and the other party did not make such a petition. We see by this that if both persons concerned in such a matter were to petition the Cosmic, and each asked for a favorable decision, that the Cosmic would have to decide and impress the hesitating judge with what is his duty, and what is proper in the points in question.

As to borrowing money, many other things must be taken into consideration. The Cosmic is

not loathe to aid in the matter of borrowing, provided the motive back of the desire to borrow is
right, and the person who wants to borrow has
proved to the Cosmic and to others that he is one
who keeps his word and repays whatever he promises to repay. Again we realize that the Cosmic
will not aid in any injustice or in any matter that
will be unfair or injurious to another person. If,
therefore, you are attempting to borrow money
without having any real necessity for the money,
or, if a real necessity exists, without having any
ideas as to where, how, or when you will be able
to secure sufficient money to repay what you borrow, you can rest assured that the Cosmic is not
going to aid you in the matter. If, on the other
hand, in your previous transactions of small or
large amounts, you have always repaid what you
borrowed, always given back what has been loaned
to you, always met your just obligations with
every endeavor to fulfill what you have promised
to do, then you may be sure that the Cosmic will
aid you if there is a real need for the money you
are seeking. You cannot go to the Cosmic with
a vague hope that the borrowed money will be

repaid some time in some way, or with the idea that when it comes time for you to pay the money back to the person you have borrowed it from, you will appeal again to the Cosmic to deliver some more money to you in order that you may square your left hand, while you get ready to hold out your right hand for something more.

In seeking the aid of the Cosmic in borrowing money, it is presumed that you have in mind some person or place from which to borrow the money, that this person or place can loan it to you without injury to itself, and that you will make it a regular business transaction, clean-cut, and of the proper ethical form. With these points being true, you may then visualize the amount of money and the person and place from which you desire to borrow it. By concentrating upon such visualization three times a day you may count upon the Cosmic's help, provided, of course, you have made the regular earthly, physical, material appeal to the person or place, in addition to concentrating upon the Cosmic. It is not to be presumed that you may want to borrow some money from Mr. Smith and without ever letting Mr. Smith know you want the money, proceed to concentrate upon the Cosmic and ask the Cosmic to urge Mr. Smith to walk to your house and hand you the money, as though he were being forced to do it by the Cosmic. In all cases of borrowing, it is proper that you should make your appeal and request to the persons first, in a regular way, and acquaint them with the knowledge that you wish to borrow from them.

In attempting to borrow money from anyone, it is always advisable to use the utmost frankness and be extremely specific. To go to any man or woman, or institution, such as a bank or loan association, and ask for an indefinite amount of money, and in a way that shows that you are not familiar with what you want, and why you want it, will surely bring a negative result. And to be evasive in your answers will likewise jeopardize your success with any person or institution, just as it would with the Cosmic.

It is understood, of course, that the borrowing of money has become an ethical process in the world today, and many institutions and persons earn more money by loaning money. Our banks in America and elsewhere would cease to exist, and would go out of business if they did not loan money, as well as receive money from persons who put it on deposit in their care. A bank's only real excuse for existing is to receive money from depositors, and loan and invest that money in many ways, so that it will earn an income and produce more money. Many persons have money which they are willing and ready to loan under certain conditions, and such persons demand the utmost frankness and security.

In talking to the manager of one of the largest loan associations in America, he frankly told me that in their institution, where millions of dollars are loaned through their various branches every month, seventy-five per cent of the money is loaned, not on security, on notes, or on written paper, but on character. He said that while interviewing persons who wish to borrow money from them, and while having the questionnaire or question sheet filled out, the manager who is doing the interviewing at each one of these branches studies the person who is applying for the loan and reaches a decision in most cases from his study of character, and the money is loaned on the strength of the person's apparent stability and integrity. Of course, they also secure signatures and notes in the form of security, as a means of legal protection, but this manager frankly told me that such papers usually prove of no value whatsoever if there is no character or integrity back of the person doing the borrowing.

With this loan association, and with individuals all over the world, the hesitating, evasive borrower is given a negative answer in the mind of the person who has the money to loan, long before he speaks a word. The shifting eye, the hesitating voice, the indefinite explanation are earmarks of irresponsibility. When a person is quite positive and definite about why he wants the borrowed money, what he intends to do with it, and when he expects to pay it back, he finds a ready listener and ready money at his disposal. Most loan associations, banks, and persons who make a business of loaning money, are interested not only in the character of the borrower, but in the purpose for which the money is being borrowed. You can well imagine that neither a bank nor an individual would loan money to a person when that person says he wants to use it for gambling or betting at the race track, or for some other wild, illegal, or irregular form of speculation. Nor will such an organization loan money to a man in very moderate circumstances who wants the money to buy an automobile for pleasure. If that same man could show, however, that he needed the money to buy a small automobile truck in order to increase his business, or efficiently carry on his business, the money would be loaned for that specific purpose.

Everyone who has money to loan would hesitate to loan it to another to buy luxuries instead of necessities, and even household furniture, radios, and pianos are not included among the necessities. Clothing, food, the payment of rent, doctors' bills, the purchase of material for business, the investment of money into a growing and successful business proposition, the buying of railroad tickets to go to some point for business purposes, the buying of a home that is in a good location and is a good real estate investment, or other real estate purposes, are generally considered good mo-

tives for borrowing. To borrow money to educate a son or daughter, when there is reason to
believe that the parents will benefit by such education, and will be able to pay back the money, is
sometimes considered a good investment, but to
borrow money in order to enjoy a pleasure trip to
Egypt would be considered a risk, and at the same
time show that the person asking for the money
has little or no sense of business values and money
values.

Every firm or individual who loans money expects interest at the legal rate, or sometimes a little
higher. Very few persons are willing to take their
money out of the bank where it is earning four
or five per cent, and loan it to someone on the
promise of securing six per cent. The risk of loaning their money, plus the trouble of collecting
it, and the delays in having the installments met
promptly so that they would bear the proper
amount of interest, would more than offset the
benefit of an additional one per cent or two per
cent that they would secure from the borrower
instead of from the bank. So you must be prepared, in many cases, to pay more than the usual

rate of interest if you expect anyone to take a risk of this kind.

You need not feel that you are hurting your integrity or your standing in a social or business way by borrowing money, for many of the larger firms, the most successful business institutions, and the most prosperous individuals find it necessary to borrow money from their banks or from other persons at times, in order to increase their business or carry on a special deal in an emergency. What will hurt you more than borrowing money is failure to keep your promises regarding the payments on the return of it. What will injure your prospects of securing borrowed money more than anything else is the record of the manner in which you have lived and spent money when you have had it. A person who has had plenty of money, or sufficient money, at one time or another, and has squandered it, and has used it for drinking and for habits that are not wholesome, or for purposes that are not ethical, cannot expect to have others loan him more money. All these things are taken into consideration by the Cosmic, as well as by the mortal mind of man.

Therefore, in asking the Cosmic's cooperation, you must be absolutely sure that you are appealing with "clean hands." And you must have made your solicitations to the persons or institutions in the usual way, before you ask the Cosmic to help bring it about. The Cosmic is not going to conduct a telegraph office or a telegraphic system, and communicate with banks all over the country and tell them you want some money, and that one of them should loan it to you. But the Cosmic will help, if you are worthy and deserving of the loan, to impress upon the minds of the persons who can make the loan that you are worthy, and that the loan should be made, and will even go to the extent of urging them to make the loan more quickly or with less delay than usual.

In securing money for business purposes, always be sure that your business is one that is really paying, or capable of being made into a paying business. Dreams and speculative propositions are neither supported by the Cosmic nor financed by financiers. I have had men come to me years ago with ideas for the building of airplanes that were simply so ridiculous that one could hardly keep from laughing, and yet they expected someone to loan them thousands of dollars to build what was only a dream in their minds. If you have not made airplanes or worked on them, or have not done any flying in them, you have no right to think that you have a new idea about them, and that the idea should be financed by someone else. On the other hand, if you have aided in the manufacture of airplanes for a number of years, and have had considerable experience in flying them, and have discovered through experimentation, building of models, and testing, that you have a better idea about airplanes than others, you can rest assured that there will be many who can help you finance it. If you are a blacksmith, and have succeeded in being a good blacksmith, but now have an idea that you would like to open a drug store, because you believe there is more money in it, do not expect anyone to agree with you in your decision and put up the money to start you in the drug store business, unless it is someone who does not care what happens to his money, or what kind of experience you get out of it. But if you have been a good druggist and you wish to move into a new section and open a better drug store, where there is little competition, and every possibility of succeeding, you will find there are others ready to help you in the plan.

You cannot expect, either, to raise money to find sunken fortunes or missing gold. Undoubtedly thousands of ships containing jewels and gold worth fabulous fortunes have sunk in the sea in the past centuries. Undoubtedly these fortunes at the bottom of the seas, and not far from shore lines, could be salvaged, so far as the value of the things is concerned. But despite the fact that dozens of companies have been incorporated and formed to salvage these fortunes, and people have risked their money in investing in such salvage schemes, not one of them has ever succeeded in securing enough gold from the interior of some of these sunken ships to pay back the money he has borrowed, or has secured on investments. If you have some such wild ideas as these, do not expect any person of sound mind and sound business principles to finance the scheme for you. If you want to buy a farm and a nice little home on it, you will find someone who will help you with it, provided you can show you are a farmer, and not a bookkeeper. On the other hand, if you are a good bookkeeper or an accountant, or a dressmaker, or a watchmaker, you can secure money to help you improve the work you are in, provided you are honest, skillful, and dependable. And the Cosmic will help you in all these legitimate propositions, and silently smile, by negative action, at the scheming ideas of the impractical dreamer.

Chapter VI

THE ATTAINMENT OF WEALTH

ONTENTED in life, indeed, is the person who has no desire for the attainment of wealth. Few there are who do not have this desire to some extent, or who do not express it in some form.

Fortunately, all of us do not measure wealth by the same standard, nor do we desire richness in the same measure. Regardless of what we may possess, or what may be our privilege to enjoy, most of us seek some things in abundance, and that abundance may be our wealth.

Before taking up several points of a practical process, which will enable us to bring wealth into our possession, let us consider what constitutes wealth for the average human being. It may be trite to say that one man's wealth may be another man's burden, or that what one person cherishes as a rare and costly gift may be of no value to another; but, it is true, nevertheless, and there seems to be but one material thing which, by common acceptance by persons of all minds, constitutes wealth—and that is money. However, there is one immaterial possession or blessing which most of us enjoy, and which, by common consent also, is considered as the equal of wealth in any form—and that is health.

The power of money in the world today is unquestionably a curse with those who do not know its real place in the scheme of things, and who cannot relegate it to its proper place.

In a preceding chapter, I said I would speak about money, and this is my opportunity. If there were no money in the world, or no material thing that represented wealth, or had the power of fictitious valuation, health and the freedom of existence would constitute the real wealth of every human being.

In the proper scheme of things, man should labor to assist in producing and materializing the created things of the world's requirements. There should be no other motive for his daily labor, no other incentive for his dreaming and planning, than to assist in the carrying out of God's constructive work. He should feel that he will share in the

world's blessings, with all beings. He should know
that of what he assists in producing a portion will
be enjoyed by him, and a portion enjoyed by his
children, who are too young or incapable of assist-
ing in producing. He should know that unless he
contributes to the universal effort, and takes his
proper place in the creative world, he cannot hope
to enjoy the blessings of the universe, nor to indulge in the beneficent joys resulting from the
labors of others.

This is no socialistic plea, nor doctrine of poli-
tics. It is merely the mystical viewpoint of life as
it should be. But man has learned that he may enjoy life's blessings and indulge in the necessities as
he understands them, by buying them with fictitious symbols which have the power to secure those
things which have not been earned or paid for.
Thus, one man may labor diligently, and even to
great extremes, to sustain life in his own body and
to provide the bare necessities for his wife and
children, while another man may labor not at all,
nor produce, nor even plan or create, but live a
life of laziness and indolence; and yet, through an
inherited possession or unfair scheming, is able to

buy with the gold that he has not mined from the earth, or with metals that he has not labored to extract, or jewels that he has not physically produced, such luxuries, privileges, and such abundant supplies as permit him to flaunt his extravagant wealth, while others cry for the things that he casts aside.

It is unquestionably true that the average man or woman who finds life devoid of the necessities or luxuries, and whose longing is for wealth in some form, is a victim of the man-made process of rewarding labor with money, or compensating effort with symbols of fictitious value. If money were not the thing with which the necessities and luxuries of life could be secured, then few indeed would be without that which they needed most. It is neither the sluggard or indolent man, nor the man who need not work or labor, who most generally petitions the Cosmic or prays to the God of all beings to aid him in attaining wealth. It is the man who is laboring industriously, consistently, and fairly; it is the man—or woman—who is devoting most of the daytime hours to laboring by the sweat of the brow, and by the torment of the body; it is the one who is striving in every honorable way, and against seemingly insurmountable obstacles, to earn and deserve the necessities of life. He it is who finds the battle against poverty and sorrow a most difficult one, and who, without losing faith or hope, and without giving up his tiresome efforts, appeals to the Cosmic and to the higher laws of the universe for aid and assistance in securing for himself, and those dependent upon him, that which will bring them joy with their health, and happiness with their necessities. Such a man seeks to attain wealth, and his wealth is a wealth that is deserved, and his desires and petitions should be answered.

Among the practical considerations which we must analyze at this time are the facts that material wealth does not always bring into our lives the real wealth we seek, and that very often we unconsciously associate the money standard with our thoughts of our needs.

In speaking with hundreds of men and women, who believed that the attainment of wealth was their real ambition, we have found that in nearly every case money was desired in order to secure or purchase or even attract, other things which it was believed could not be secured or attracted except through the power of money. In the preceding chapter, I have tried to show that petitioning for money in most cases was not the right way to bring about the ultimate desires within one's heart. I would like to show at this time, however, that the petitioning for wealth—abundant wealth —may be a proper procedure, and that the desire for it may be a proper thought.

Among my intimate associates in the business world, was that master of finance and big business, Mr. Arthur Stillwell, who built more railroads in America than any other living being, and whose power on Wall Street at one time was so great that his voice on the convention floor at the time of the selection of a national candidate for the presidency turned the tide of big business in its ramifications toward political goals. I have had the pleasure of being the adviser to Mr. Stillwell in many and great business propositions. Some of them were cast aside after brief consideration, often upon my own private recommendation, while others were developed and enlarged into successful national operations, solely through the personal effort it was my pleasure to institute. Mr. Stillwell was a man of remarkable mental and psychic development, and I am glad to note that he has published in some national magazines, articles reviewing his mental and psychological contests with big business deals and the victories that have come into his life—many a time through the application of the mystical laws which were demonstrated to him in the secret sessions we held while I was his silent partner during the course of a number of years.

Mr. Stillwell's idea of wealth, however, was not that wealth which gradually accumulated for him in the vaults of Wall Street, or even in the holdings in international marts. His idea of great wealth was the wealth of character, and of mental power. He considered that there was no power in the world as strong, as mighty, as indefatigable in its processes of overcoming the obstacles of life as the creative power of mind. His daily petition to the universal Mind and Consciousness was a prayer for the continuance of health and especially of that power which was developing in his mental faculties.

On many occasions, when Mr. Stillwell tele-
phoned me late in the night to go to his private
office in New York, he greeted me with a joyous
grip and a hearty smile, and the exuberant claim
that "I am truly wealthy tonight, for I have a
great idea!" And as we would discuss his idea, I
could not help but note that he enjoyed the thought
which he held. He cherished it like a loving child,
not because he could see that the idea would some
day produce money for himself and others, but because the idea was a thing alive with possibilities,
and because it could be visualized and matured and
eventually materialized into a vibrating magnetic
demonstration of mental laws. There was not always a selfish interest in these ideas of his, for I
have spent long hours with him discussing an idea
which both of us realized we would have to pass
on to another to turn into commercial form, for
neither one of us would have the time nor the interest in developing the idea along business channels. But we could see in the idea a germ, and we
could see this germ conscious and active with life
and possibility, and often such ideas were passed
over to his associates, some of whom were con-

nected with the Standard Oil Company, or with other large industries whose executives we were acquainted with, and whose planners and builders were also men who appreciated the value of ideas, and had the true standard of wealth in their consciousness.

The man today who has a good idea, a workable idea, and a creative mind in which that idea can be mastered and visualized, is a man who has wealth, boundless wealth, potent wealth. The man who has money, who has jewels, who has gold and silver in sufficiency or in abundance, but who has not the creative power to use such wealth, is not rich but poor indeed.

In petitioning the Cosmic, or in using the psychological processes to bring wealth into one's personal environment, the less thought given to wealth as represented by money or gold or silver, the more quickly will the petitioner attract to himself the ways and means of attaining that which will really constitute his wealth in this life.

First of all, those who believe they are deprived of life's necessities, or think that they lack the abundance which should be theirs, should seek **to** build up the greatest wealth and blessing that is within their reach, and that is health. Perfect health, with the harmonious functioning of all the inner faculties, cooperating with the functioning faculties of the consciousness outside of man, is one of the greatest blessings that man may possess. When such health is in the body, the mind is keen and alert, and the creative powers of the Divine Mind working through the mortal mind are active, and productive. Man is then able to direct and control the obstacles that stand between him and the attainment of his desires. He is able to appeal to the minds of others without doubt and without hesitancy. He is truly the master of his life, and the captain of his ship, and it is just as possible for him to steer his ship of fate and his life of destiny toward the goal of his dreams, and toward the pot at the end of the rainbow, as it is for the experienced navigator scientifically to bring his ship to the distant point on any horizon.

The next great blessing is that of receptivity. To receive, one must give. And as we give, we receive. It is the law of compensation. No man as yet has successfully avoided this law, nor found a way to contest and negate it. Man's mind must become receptive to the intuitional impressions sent forth by the Cosmic; it must become receptive to the still, small voice within that seeks to guide and direct all of man's actions, all of his thinking and planning. Man must become receptive to the inspirational urges of the universal Mind. He must become receptive to the cries and the needs, the desires and the wishes, of the mass mind of humanity, so that he may hear the pleas of the individuals, and the hopes of the groups of men and women who are sending out into the universal space their creative ideas, seeking assistance in their fulfillment and materialization. The receptive mind must be able to sense what another needs, as well as what is needed by the self. The receptive mind must be attuned to the divine Consciousness, that it may have the unlimited wisdom, the infinite knowledge, and the universal apprehension of things as they really are. To be receptive, one must be productive. One must contribute in order to expect anything in return. Life will give back precisely what one puts into it, and in a greater measure.

Let him who seeks great wealth beware of seeking gold, unless it be to materialize it into the beautiful things of life, symbolized by the very nature of the metal. Let him who would be wealthy guard himself against seeking for money. For money may come into the hand and pass out again without ever leaving its impress of joy, or a realization of the dreams that sought its coming.

In the home and in the business, let each man and each woman daily, nightly, or at every possible opportunity, petition the Cosmic for wealth of health, the wealth of mind power, the wealth of joy in living, the wealth of contentment that comes from adjusting ourselves to the conditions that surround us, and then slowly improving them. To the wealth of happiness that exists in our lives if we will but discover it; to the wealth of peace that the universe affords all its beings; to the wealth of life itself that permits us to know what we are, and that we are who we are—such petitions for wealth as these, followed by prayers of thankfulness for what we have, will daily attune the individual to the abundant wealth of the universe, and each will soon find that affluence and prosperity, health and happiness, material blessings and spiritual benedictions, are flowing freely and bountifully into the filling cup of life.

Then each one of us will know what really constitutes wealth, and what is meant by the mystic when he seeks the attainment of wealth.

CHAPTER VII

SEEKING EMPLOYMENT

E MUST NOT overlook the fact that not all who seek aid in business matters are seeking for money, for speculation or investment, nor even any specific thing in life's journey. Many ask only for an opportunity to serve, and to earn all of the necessities of life, plus a few of its luxuries.

In other words, not all are looking for large sums of money, or for homes, or for fulfillment of great dreams. Perhaps most of those who appeal to us for help are those who are seeking to secure better positions in the business world, or for opportunities whereby they may improve their employment.

Since women have entered the business world, conditions are considerably different than they were a few years ago. There was a time when the employment of a woman in any part of a business institution was considered as an indication that the employer was seeking to secure services at a lower wage standard than that demanded by a man. This was because the average woman in the business world was receiving a salary much smaller than could be offered to a man of the same age in the same capacity. This situation placed a handicap, in some respects, in the path of the man who was well qualified to fill a good position, but who had to demand higher wages because of family and other financial obligations. In other words, the race between men and women for positions in the business world was not a fair one, for the woman had the advantage of being able to offer her services at a lower scale. This put competition between men and women on a basis of salary difference.

Today, however, the average woman in the business world is receiving the same salary as the man, and very few business men think of employing anyone in any important position because of any economy in the matter of salary. The outstanding qualification is tending to be that of experience and capability. And, in the matter of capability, woman is rapidly proving herself to be the equal of man in many capacities. Therefore, the contest between men and women today in seeking positions is a contest of qualifications, not one of salary.

I know thousands of business men who frankly say that when they have a vacancy which calls for a capable person to fill, they care little whether the successful applicant is a man or a woman, and usually the matter of salary is settled in the mind of the employer before he decides upon the applicant. And he does not think of offering a lower salary to the applicant because she happens to be a woman.

I know there are men who will disagree with me because they feel that often they have been removed from a position to be supplanted by a woman, or have been unsuccessful in securing a position, because the successful applicant was a woman; and in each instance they have felt that the woman's only advantage with the employer was that of salary. If you are a man, and you hold such ideas as these, you are prejudicing your mind, and you are building up the first great psychological obstacle to your success in securing a new position, or in securing promotion in your present position.

Too many employees today fail to realize that the business world now demands efficiency. Capability is the standard by which every successful business gauges its employees. I am not speaking of new and inexperienced employers, who are starting in business for the first time and employing help for the first time in their lives. Such inexperienced persons may assume that female help can be secured at a lower scale of wages, with the same efficiency as male help at a higher scale, and they show favoritism toward female applicants. But such business men will learn sooner or later that they receive in return just such efficiency and capability as they pay for, and that it is a serious mistake to use the standard of wages between the sexes as a basis for selection.

In every successful business, selections for new positions or for promotions are made on the basis of experience and special capability. And if you want to be successful in your business career, you will avoid seeking positions with new firms and with inexperienced employers who do not have such a standard for the selection of employees.

For the Home and Business

Of course there are certain qualifications possessed by women which men do not possess, and men undoubtedly possess other qualifications which women do not possess. We were accustomed to think that women or young ladies made the very best secretaries and stenographers, but this, too, has been found to be an arbitrary decision, not based upon any fact so far as capability is concerned. And we have been accustomed to think that in certain lines of business, women were out of place. All this has been changed in recent years, and I can assure you that it is not uncommon for one to find in some of the largest institutions, corporations, and nation-wide business propositions, women holding executive or other positions that one would naturally expect to find filled by men.

It is, therefore, quite evident that when a man or woman seeks a new position, or promotion in any business, the idea that the difference in sex makes any difference in capability or in the employer's mind, should be immediately dismissed; and the seeker for employment should at once begin to analyze himself and his capabilities with no other thought in mind than that he must discover, or she must discover, how well qualified he or she is as an individual to fill the position being sought.

All these remarks are preliminary to some of the important things I would impress upon the mind of the seeker for employment. In interviewing hundreds of persons each year who are seeking new positions or better positions, and who tell me of their failure to secure what they seek, I find that they generally have a tendency to blame their failure upon certain preconceived ideas or false beliefs which they have established in their minds.

Foremost among the false beliefs is the idea that "pull," or personal influence of some kind, is a very important factor. I have found from my own experience, and in conversation with many thousands of big business men, that the only way in which they have ever noticed that "pull" or influence brought someone into their employ was through the assistance of another in letting someone else know that there was a vacancy. In other words, assuming that Mr. Jones was contemplating engaging a new secretary or a new department manager, and that he expressed his intention to some friend, if that friend knew of a very capable and efficient person and told him to call on Mr. Jones, and ask for the position, and if he seemed to be as capable as Mr. Jones expected his new employee to be, the probability is that he would secure the position. And in this way it might be said that some "pull" or influence enabled the employee to secure a very fine position. But you will note that I have distinctly said that *if* the employee was as capable and efficient as the employer expected, then the employee would secure the position. I know that business men will not engage an employee of inferior qualifications or capabilities just because that person comes well recommended from some friend, or has some "pull" or influence with some acquaintance, with the employer, or with the business concern. In fact, I know of thousands of instances where influence and so-called "pull" have tried to place an unqualified or partially qualified person in an important position, but when the employer interviewed the applicant, and found him unworthy of the position, the influence of friend or family, or even the political or financial "pull" of

important members of the firm, has failed to secure the position for that applicant.

Of course it is but natural for an employee to
think that he is as well qualified for many positions
as those who are employed with him in any business concern, and it is natural also for him to feel
that when one of them is promoted over his head
some influence has been brought to bear in making the selection. Natural though that feeling
may be, it is generally wrong, and the employee
who has failed to be promoted, or who has failed
to secure an expected position, and who blames
his failure on influence and "pull," is generally
doing himself an injustice, as well as doing an
injustice to the successful applicant.

The moment we attribute our failure in securing
anything in life to the exterior influences which we
imagine exist, we shut the door against self-analysis
and fail to learn a very valuable lesson.

The man, or woman, who fails in securing a desired position, or a desired favor at the hands of
another, should turn that failure into a very valuable steppingstone to rise higher. He, or she,
should immediately proceed to find why the other

person succeeded and why he, or she, failed, and if this examination and analysis is properly conducted and conscientiously carried on, it will probably enable the unsuccessful applicant to discover how he, or she, may improve and prepare for a more successful attempt.

The average business firm in America today promotes its employees from the lower ranks to the higher ranks, as each employee demonstrates his mastership in his present position, and his possible capability for a higher one. But there are limits to such promotions in many lines of business. There is often a point in the ladder of promotion for every employee when he cannot be promoted higher than he is, regardless of his present efficiency and capability, and regardless of the fact that there are openings for employees higher up in the business. Therefore, when an employee finds that he has reached a point in the business where he is situated in which he can no longer secure promotion, and finds others brought in from the outside to fill positions above him that he thinks he can fill, he should not attribute the engagement of others as due to influence, nor even feel that his failure to be promoted is an indication of in-capability on his part. He should try to have a frank talk with his employer and discover whether he has reached the height of his efficiency with that firm, or whether he has failed in showing special capability for promotion.

The one thing that warrants employers in pro-moting employees is the spirit of service. The man who gives only as much time and labor and thought to his work as he is paid for, is sure to find at the end of the year that he is being paid only for what he is giving. The employee who feels that he is engaged and paid for doing eight hours' work a day, and that the giving of a ninth hour should be compensated for as extra labor, is one who will find eventually that promotions do not come his way, and even increases in salary are delayed or refused. On the other hand, the em-ployee who tries to show that he is anxious to help in every department of the business, and specialize in none, and willing to hurry through his assigned work in order to make his willingness to work in other departments quite evident to his employer, is apt to make the employer feel that the employee is not giving as elaborate and careful attention to his assigned work as he should.

I have actually seen employees who were busy helping in so many departments, and trying to make themselves useful in more ways than they were engaged to be, lose their positions in a few months because the employer felt that they were not limiting their thinking and their industry to the assigned work, and therefore were neglecting it in some phases, or failing to find in their particular work, the possibilities of enlargements and extra efforts that were close at hand.

But it is natural that an employer will appreciate every special effort, and every extended endeavor that an employee puts into the business, regardless of the time-clock or the salary being paid.

I have heard so many employees say that if their employer would give them a little interest in the business, or even fractional percentage of the profits being accrued, they would be willing to put some personal interest in the work at hand. The trouble with this argument is that if the employee thought it was possible for him to put some personal interest into the business, to such an extent that he would do his work better and more rapidly, or more completely, then he should have put that interest into his work long before he expected the employer to compensate him for it by giving him a share of the profits. Let an employer discover in his own peculiar way that you have more than merely a salary interest in his business, and he will gladly see to it that you are compensated accordingly. The demonstration must begin on your part, and not on the part of the employer.

Another one of the things which are responsible for many employees' losing their positions, or failing to be promoted, is the lack of loyalty to the employer or the institution wherein he is employed. Taking time off to seek better positions, or stealing occasional minutes to interview someone about a position in another firm, or ways and means for securing promotion, have caused more employees to lose their positions than any other single thing. An employer has a right to believe that you should be so loyal to your position and your employer that while you are working for him and with him, you have no thoughts regarding your own personal interest, your own personal affairs, or your own personal dreams. To discover an employee seeking another position outside of the firm is a signal to any employer to release that employee and secure another one. The employer does not want to be caught off guard by having you suddenly resign and leave your position unfilled, and your work unattended to. If he believes that you are seeking another position or seeking to make some change, even within his own business, he is apt to feel that you are undependable and not loyal.

For the same reason, thousands of persons seeking employment fail to secure desirable positions for which they may be well qualified in a mental or physical way. Such persons frankly tell their prospective employers that they have worked for a number of different firms, but have left each one because they wanted to improve themselves or secure a better position. This confession to an employer means that the applicant is not dependable, and that to engage him today may mean losing him a month from now. And if there is any one thing that harasses, bothers, annoys, and infuriates an employer as to help, it is to seek new employees constantly, interview them, and have them trained in their positions.

On the other hand, the employee who thinks that he will take advantage of this fact and demands that he be promoted or given an increase in salary so as to avoid vacating his position and causing the employer the trouble of seeking a new employee, is proceeding very foolishly, and against his own best interests. Any employer would rather go through all of the tiresome procedure of seeking and interviewing new applicants, and having them broken into new positions, than to be subjected to such coercion.

From a mystical or Cosmic point of view, loyalty to your employer is the keynote to success for those who are employed, and such loyalty is not only of the physical body, but of the mind and heart. And it is not something that exists only during eight hours of presence in an office or building, but is twenty-four hours long each day.

Every employer knows that an employee in his business may be worth more to his competitor or to someone else in a similar line of business, who needs a similar person, than the employee is to him. And when the employee decides that he has an opportunity to use his experience to secure another position with a competitive firm, he is being disloyal to his present employer and disloyal to himself. The chances are that the new employer will remember that he left a trusting employer to come to him, and he will be wary of the employee's faithfulness. Cosmically speaking, the inexperienced employee who does this sort of thing is bringing a Karmic condition upon himself which will bring him failure and discontent for a long time.

Let me cite a practical illustration of Cosmic Karma in this regard. An employee, just graduated from a business course, applies for a position as clerk in a corporation. The employer needs another worker, and engages the applicant and proceeds to use his own time and the time of a number of other employees to train and educate the new employee so that he will become efficient and worthy. The employer is paying the employee a nominal salary to start with, and the chances are that in ninety-nine cases out of one hundred, he receives more salary each week for the first six months he is in his position, than he earns. According to the law of averages in every business, the new employee is probably receiving seventy-five per cent more salary than he is actually worth, when it is taken into consideration that the employer's time and the time of a number of other employees must be used to help him understand and master his duties. The employer, however, counts on the future months and years of that employee to earn for him that which he has not earned during the first six months, and to make up for the money he has received during the six months of preparation. But after the first six months are past, the employee who thinks he has earned every cent he has received, demands an increase in salary. The employer realizes that instead of now having an opportunity of making up for the overpayment that has been given to the employee during the preceding six months, he must face the situation of paying more money and continuing to lose money, or lose the employee and engage another one. In the employee's mind, however, there is this one thought: That he can now go into the office of some other concern, and with the six months' experience he has had, at the expense of the other firm, he is ready to receive a slightly higher salary in his new position. In other words, he is ready to take advantage of the experience he has had at someone else's expense, and turn it to profit for himself, ungrateful and unmindful of the obligation he owes to his present employer. Being refused an increase in salary, he leaves his present employer and goes to another concern.

A record carefully kept of a thousand employees doing this sort of thing has shown that at the end of a year these employees were again out of positions, and in two years their changes in positions, with periods of unemployment, showed that they had earned less in the two years through their many changes than they would have earned had they remained in their first positions and secured a raise at the end of the first year. Furthermore, their continual changing of positions has given them a record which no employer values, and they soon find themselves among the army of unemployed, and disgruntled, discontented, and suspicious of the entire employment system.

In seeking a position, therefore, be sure that you are well qualified, that you are ready to give it your loyalty and entire support, and that you are willing to work and labor with the concern for such a length of time as will enable it to secure from your services such reward as will make increases profitable to them and to you.

If you are seeking promotion in your present concern or position, you will be sure of securing it if you give less thought to the promotion or to the possibility that lies before you, and more thought during your business hours to the work you have at hand.

Let your thinking about your advancements or changes in position occur during your hours of relaxation while you are at home; and rather than concentrate upon your employer's mind with all kinds of silly demands that he grant your recent request, concentrate your mind for a moment or two on yourself, and see if you can find how you can go into your present position the next morning and do your work a little better, or improve the affairs of your business for your employer and thereby attract his mind to your desires.

In appealing to the Cosmic, or through any mystical laws, for advancement, promotion, or the securing of a new position, be sure that you have in mind a definite position along a definite line of effort of which you are capable, and in which you can demonstrate efficiency.

In interviewing an employer regarding a change or a new position, follow the suggestions given in the next chapter about interviewing and selling, for you must sell yourself. But in addition to following those suggestions, be sure that you make it plain to your employer that you are not offering him just your eight hours of physical labor each day, but you are offering him your best mental services, your loyalty, your interest, and that degree of efficiency which he may expect.

With all of these suggestions in mind, and with the advice given in future chapters, you should be able to make your life as an employee just as successful and profitable to you as any business in which you might engage yourself and become an employer.

Chapter VIII

IMPRESSING OTHERS

HERE are certain psychological principles which may be used and applied very efficiently, even by those who have not taken a thorough course in the subject of psychology, or who have not had long experience with the intricate principles involved.

The most careful use of these psychological principles—in connection with that of impressing the mind of another person, and the art of making the proper impression—is very important to those who are attempting to convey a message of a definite nature.

Now whether you are trying to sell some merchandise to a person, or sell yourself, it is absolutely necessary that you create in the mind of your prospective buyer a duplicate of the picture that you have in your mind. Really it is the art of thought transference, but instead of being accomplished by the process of mental telepathy exclusively, you have the additional advantage of

[139]

using words and using some other psychological laws which I will explain.

With some persons, the most difficult thing in the world is to talk to another and talk so impressively or so efficiently that the right message is conveyed. Many persons find it more convenient and certainly more efficient to write letters than to talk, and I have known hundreds of successful salesmen who did all their selling by correspondence, and who were eminently successful. However, the moment they faced a prospective buyer and attempted to say in words what they had been accustomed to saying in letters, they became self-conscious, wobbly in their concentration, and weak in their impressiveness.

If you are one of those persons who can write a strong letter and present your proposition by mail better than you can in person, you certainly have an advantage and I question whether it will pay you to attempt to change your methods. But if you are in a position where you must face your prospective buyer, or where personal interviews are absolutely necessary, then there are certain principles which you can use and which will make your work more sure of results.

As I have said above, whether you are selling merchandise, or applying for a position, or seeking favors or benefits of any kind, you are either selling some material thing or selling yourself. And in either case, you must create in the mind of your prospective buyer, or the person you are interviewing, that sort of impression and that sort of picture which you have in your own mind.

Now you cannot send a telegram by walking into a telegraph office and telling the clerk that you want to say something, but do not know what it is you wish to say. Neither can you convey an impression from your mind to another if you do not have a clear picture in your mind to begin with. That which you wish to have your prospective buyer build up in his mind, must be so concrete and definite in your own that you never have to hesitate a moment in the process of transferring the impression from your own mind to his mind.

On the other hand, you cannot send a telegram of congratulations to anyone by walking into the office and filing with the clerk a telegram of sympathy and sorrow. You cannot convey to the mind of another person an impression of positive affirmation and of whole-hearted conviction, if in your own mind the impression you have there is weak or negative, or the opposite of what you wish to convey.

In other words, you cannot face your interviewer and glibly talk, positively, about the goodness and merits of something you wish to sell, while in your own mind there is a doubt about the goodness of the thing, and a conviction that the thing has no merit. You can train your lips to speak a lie, and you can glibly juggle your words so that you are conveying a double meaning, but you cannot trick your mind into forgetting the facts it knows and creating momentarily a false picture in agreement with the false words you are speaking.

The average business man who is accustomed to dealing with salesmen or interviewing persons who wish to seek favors, benefits, or assistance, has become keenly sensitive to the vibrating impressions from the mind of the speaker, and I wish to tell you frankly that I know of thousands of such business men who secretly admit that they seldom pay as much attention to the words being spoken by their interviewer as they do to the thought impressions they are receiving in between his words.

I know from my own experience, and from the experience of many business men who have discussed this matter with me, that very often the business man reaches a conclusion as to what he is going to do long before the salesman or the interviewer is half through his talking. Often after the first half-dozen words are spoken by the salesman or the interviewer, the business man who is listening has received direct from the mind of the talker an impression that all is not as it seems, and that the man is attempting to fool him, or trick or deceive him, by his talking. Under such circumstances, the business man immediately decides that he will *not* buy and will *not* grant the requests being asked, and nothing that the salesman or the interviewer says changes that impression.

The very opposite of this is also true. The average busy man in big business will often interrupt a salesman or an interviewer by saying: "All right, I will accept," or "I agree," or "I will grant what you wish." It would appear that he has made up his mind before the interviewer or talker has half explained his proposition. Others who witness such things as this think it is due to the fact that the business man has some hunch or some intuitive way of deciding what he should do. This is not true, however. He has simply received from the interviewer's mind an impression that reached him before the interviewer had spoken a half-dozen words. Busy business men have little time for long discussions and long interviews. If they can get the impressions from the salesman's mind mentally, in a moment, they would rather have it that way than wait a half-hour to get it through a long series of complex statements and descriptive explanations.

From all of this you will see that the salesman who attempts, nowadays, to sell something that has no real merit, or in which he has little faith or confidence, is lost unless he is going to try to sell it to ignorant, uncultured, and inexperienced buyers, and even there he may fail because it must be remembered that a lack of education and a lack of culture does not prevent the human mind from being very sensitive to mental impressions. The average street hound has little culture and no education, but it is mighty sensitive in reading the auras and mental impressions of the persons who pass it by. The salesman, or anyone else, who thinks that he can take advantage of uneducated persons and untutored and unlettered minds and work a trick upon their inner intelligence, is very apt to be fooled.

In trying to sell yourself to a prospective buyer, whether it be seeking a promotion in business, a new position, or some special service you wish to render, remember that your own real opinion of yourself and of your service counts far more than the beautiful description that you will give with words, or which may be glowingly stated in a number of testimonial letters you ask him to read. If you doubt your own ability to fill the position you are seeking, if you have the least doubt in your mind about your efficiency or capability for the service you wish to render, do not think that you can buffalo your business man by egotistical statements nicely worded. Glowing promises mean very little to the business man. He naturally assumes that everyone who wants to work for him or serve him is going to try to do his best. The mere fact that you say you will do your best means nothing. He wants to know what your best really is, and if you have any doubt back in your mind as to how good that best is, he is going to discover it very soon.

Many persons are full of promises in their interviews, and then they are about as dry as the Sahara Desert when it comes to making good those promises. The most promising thing I ever heard of was a Mississippi steamboat that had a twenty-two-inch whistle, and a sixteen-inch steam boiler, and when it was ready to start away from the dock, it blew its whistle with such strong, promising tones that it exhausted its steam and moved backward.

So the first thing to do is to have the proper determination in your mind, and a very complete, definite picture of the real service you wish to render, or the true value of the goods or things you wish to sell. If you are attempting to sell merchandise, whether it be stocks and bonds or articles of commerce, be sure you are so familiar with what you are selling that not only can you answer glibly any question that is asked, but you can close your eyes and in a moment see an entire picture of the article from the time it started in its process of manufacture from the raw materials, to the last moment of its delivery.

Unless you are as familiar with that which you are offering someone else as you are with the part in your hair and the wax on your mustache, do not think that you have a clear conception of the goods at all. All the while that you are talking to your prospective buyer, he will be getting from your mind the precise picture you have in your mind, and if it is about as blurred as the motion pictures in a ten-cent motion picture house, he will get the same sort of reaction, regardless of the nice captions and glowing billboards that you paint for him to look at. Telling your prospective buyer all about what you have to offer, and at the same time having a poor picture in your mind, is like taking your buyer in front of a motion picture house and pointing out to him the attractive billboards, with all their glowing colors and screaming statements. He will tell you that the show on the inside is the thing he wants to see; therefore, your picture on the inside of yourself should be more definite and more clear-cut than what you or any poet or literary master could ever picture in words.

The next important point is to convey to your prospective buyer the fact that you are steadfast, honest, straightforward, and businesslike. Not only should your conversation be brief, your statements definite and to the point, and your whole attitude that of poise and self-confidence, but your every glance and movement should indicate a sureness and conviction that are unmistakable.

Business men do not have to have salesmen or interviewers assume an attitude of humiliation, or even of humility. They do not like the one who apologizes for taking their time to explain what he has to offer. If you are doubtful as to whether what you have to offer is of value to the man or not, do not go to see him until you are sure that it is of value. If you have the slightest feeling that you are taking up a business man's time without profit to him, then do not go near him. Unless you feel in the bottom of your heart, and in the top of your head, that your time in his presence will result in profit to him and benefit to his business, as well as any profit to yourself, do not go near him. Apologizing for your intrusion, or for the time you take, is merely another way of saying to your prospective buyer that you do not believe you are going to show him any profit in what you are presenting, and that after all he is going to be the loser if he buys or if he does not; and you may just as well save your time and his at the beginning.

Of course, if you are asking merely for a favor, wherein all the profit is for yourself and none at all for the other fellow, you may properly explain that you regret that you are taking some of his valuable time in such a selfish manner. But if you have something really of merit to offer in the way of merchandise or your own personal services, and you believe what you have to offer is of benefit or value to the other fellow, do not apologize for taking his time. Every business man is thankful to have a meritorious proposition brought to his attention, and every business man makes it his business to see and interview real live salesmen or persons who have something definite to say.

One of the sure signs of weakness in character, and inefficiency in mental ability, is the shifting eye. You will notice that the average big business man has his desk so placed in his office that the interviewer who calls to see him faces the light, while the business man has his back to the light, and has his face in the shadow. This is so that the business man can easily watch and study the changing expression of the person who is talking to him, and so that the person who is talking to him cannot see the changing expression on his face. The business man has a right to such an opportunity to examine the character and the expressions of the person who talks to him. You have no right to look upon it as being placed at a disadvantage, for if you are wise and good you will take advantage of the situation and face the light as well as his critical scrutiny, and fear nothing. In fact, you will make your face and your eyes serve your purpose, as I will explain in a few moments.

Of course it is understood that you will never go into the presence of another person seeking favors, benefits, or aid, or attempting to sell or promote any idea, if you are slovenly dressed, careless in your appearance, foul of breath, or inconsiderate and uncordial in your attitude.

Approaching your prospective buyer, you should have the positive affirmation in your mind that you are going to succeed, not by overpowering him, not by hypnotizing him, and not by having the Cosmic superinduce a state of mental coma wherein he knows nothing, says nothing, thinks nothing but what you describe in words. The Cosmic will not aid in such a method, through any law or principle of the universe. If you want to throw your prospective buyer into a state of mental aberration, you will have to do it by the charm of your personality and the goodness and greatness of your proposition.

There is one method, however, whereby you can keep your listener, whoever he may be, from letting his mind wander while you are speaking, or from coming to a conclusion too quickly. It is a method used by the most successful salesmen throughout the world, and by diplomats, detectives, judges of the court, criminologists, psychologists, and mystics. It is a method whereby you can stand before your prospective buyer or any other person and say what you have to say provided it is the truth, and make him realize it is the truth and cause him to judge your statements and your mental pictures correctly.

The method is simply this: The moment you begin speaking to the person whom you wish to convince, be sure to concentrate your two eyes all the time you are speaking on the center of his nose just between the eyebrows. That point of the nose is called the root of the nose, and if you will concentrate your gaze upon that, you will be concentrating upon the root of his attention. You will find that he will gaze back into your eyes, and he will feel the steadfast, permanent, convincing glance and mental attitude on your part. If you have to close your eyes or change your gaze from that position while talking to him, do not drop your eyes and look down to the floor or down to your lap or your hands or anything that is lower than the level of his face, but rather, shift your eyes or your glance sideways to something in the room that is on a level with his face. You can rest your eyes for a moment this way, and then bring them back to a definite view upon the root of his nose.

Do not attempt to stare with wide open eyes, as though you were trying to play the part of

Svengali and turn him into a beautiful singer.
He will become suspicious of your motives, and
you will lose out instantly. Let your eyes have
just a perfectly natural look, but merely center
them on the root of his nose instead of looking
at his watch chain or the papers on his desk, or at
your own hands or feet. Every downward glance
on your part weakens your impression. Do not
attempt to get close to your man, but stay at a
respectful distance. Talk softly and in a mono-
tone. Do not try to give emphasis to certain words
by pronouncing them loudly, for that will shock
the mind of the listener and upset the rhythm of
his thinking. Do not lean on the desk, put your
hat on his inkwell, or put your shoes on the rungs
of his chair. Do not get familiar, intimate, or personal. If you know the person in a friendly way,
reserve your personal, friendly talks for hours
after business. Make your conversations brief and
to the point.

If, when all this is done, the prospective buyer
suggests postponing a decision, do not attempt to
urge him to immediate decision. He will become
suspicious. Rome was not built in a day, and

whether he buys something from you or not, today or tomorrow, will not ruin or wreck his business. If the service or the thing you have to offer is any good at all, it will be just as good tomorrow as it is today. If you are fearful that it won't last more than twenty-four hours, and may get weak if he does not accept it right away, you will convince him that he will gain more by rejecting it than by accepting it.

Even in public speaking, and in dealing in business matters or in personal matters, be sure always to gaze at the person you are talking to with your eyes centered as instructed above. This will gain for you a mental impression of a strong, magnetic personality, and it will tend to keep your listener from wandering away mentally in a field of speculation, and you will hold him fast to your line of thought.

A thousand men have told me of a thousand instances where this formula saved the day. It may not be mystical, it may not even be psychological, but it works.

CHAPTER IX

AN UNUSUAL HELP IN NEED

(The following matter was presented originally as a lecture to a special assembly of business men. They became so enthusiastic over the possibilities of the process explained herein that for many months after the delivery of the lecture, hundreds of prominent business men in the city where the lecture was given went about their affairs using the peculiar aid explained herein, much to the amusement of their friends, but to the astonishment of those who found it efficient and of unusual benefit. Many business men are today using this process, and without any attempt to understand how or why it works, they acknowledge that Dr. Lewis revealed a truly worth-while principle to them.—Editor.)

 NE of my good friends and a member of our organization, Miss Springer, who is one of America's prominent authors, wrote a very fetching story one time entitled, "A Plea for Hypocrisy." She very capably outlined the benefit that all of us derive from some mild forms of amusing hypocrisy in our lives. I feel that before my readers are through with this chapter in my book they will believe I have written something that should be entitled, "A Plea for Superstition."

It is strange how many superstitious beliefs most of us really have, and how greatly we are affected by them. You have heard of the sane, conservative business man who laughed at the superstitious belief of his wife, regarding the raising of an umbrella in his office, and yet when he went out on the street he went out of his way to avoid walking under a ladder. In my contact with business men in all of the industries, trades, arts, and professions, I have found that nearly every one of them has some sort of superstitious belief which he indignantly refuses to have labeled as superstition, and he denies it is merely a belief. Most of them take great pains and considerable time to explain to me that the strange little conviction that is in their mind is based not upon faith but upon practical experience, and therefore, is neither a belief nor a superstition.

For the Home and Business

We are told that sailors are the most superstitious persons in the world, but I want to find a business man who is always ready and willing to start a new proposition or make a big investment on a day that happens to be Friday, the thirteenth; and I would like to find the business man who is always willing to be the thirteenth director in a new company; or the man or woman, in business, who is willing to hand over his money in a new investment just after a black cat has crossed his path. These persons will stand on a street corner for ten minutes or more, looking for a white horse right after they have seen a red-headed man, and yet deny that they have any superstitious beliefs.

However all this may be, the fact of the matter is that most of the superstitious beliefs which have come down through the ages and still grip us with their possibilities, and hold us with their potential powers, are those which are actually based upon some scientific principle. I will grant you that walking under a ladder is a risky thing at any time, especially if the ladder is not well grounded, and there is a man with a paint pot somewhere above. But there are many other superstitious beliefs or practices which deal with vital principles not so obviously connected with serious possibilities.

We hear men and women who are dealing with the important material things of life speaking of such conditions as luck and chance. While they may not go so far as to walk around their chairs four times just after a new deal of the cards, or slap the top of their heads three times after they have placed a marker on the board at the side of the roulette wheel, still they are prone to do other things which they believe will assure their success in the undertaking at hand.

Recently, the president of one of the largest coal combines in America came from Chicago to have a business consultation with me in San Jose. Whenever he finds that talking to me from New York, Pittsburgh, Chicago, or Salt Lake, on the telephone is too slow, he drops in to see me. During his last conversation, he told me how a president of one of the banks with which he does business in Chicago carries a lucky coin in his pocket, and takes hold of it and grips it tightly whenever he is dealing with an important matter, because he has found that "the vibrations from this coin bring him luck." The coal magnate smiled at the story he was telling, and then he presented me with a paper weight of a novel design for my desk, which was a duplicate of the one he had on his desk in his office in Chicago. He said it was the symbolic design of a large banking institution in New York, and that his paper weight was a reminder to him to consult them in regard to extraordinary matters because he found he had better luck in dealing with that firm than with any other. Of course he had no superstition at all!

Now the truth of the matter is that there is one strange practice used by so-called mystics, especially by business men and women who have heard of it, who have tried it first in a half-hearted way, and then found reason to pin their faith to the principle involved. I am going to explain it to you, and I suppose that the result will be that one hundred or more of you will go about your business affairs from now on doing this strange little thing, much to the amusement of your partners, and let us say to the consternation of your business enemies.

Perhaps you have heard of the peculiar trick of "crossing your fingers," and keeping them crossed while you are awaiting the result of some plan or the decision of some person who holds the key to your immediate problem. Perhaps you have thought that crossing your fingers or keeping them crossed was a superstitious practice, and perhaps it really is, I do not know, but I do know that it works. And I have found a very satisfactory explanation for the practice, and whether you accept my explanation or not, you are at perfect liberty to try the formula and cross your fingers whenever you wish, and keep them crossed as long as you like. If this practice does not bring the unusual results that others have secured, you are again at liberty to condemn the thing as a foolish superstition. On the other hand, if you secure unusual results, you are at liberty to attribute the success to the little superstitious practice.

I have found that when a man or woman has visualized and built up in the mind, a plan, a desire, or some picture representing what he or she wants from someone else, that the most difficult thing is to keep that picture in mind and have it radiate in the form of mental vibrations to the mind of the other person without interruption and without interference. I am speaking now about the man or woman who is about to interview another person, or has just completed such an interview, seeking or suggesting that certain things be done which can be done by the person being interviewed, but which may not be done because of interference, forgetfulness, or some other interruption preventing the plan from being carried out. Take, for instance, the man who goes to his banker and explains to him his need for a loan. He uses every convincing argument to show the banker that the loan is not only needed, but is a safe and businesslike proposition. The banker listens carefully and makes certain notations, but defers giving a definite answer until the next day. The man who wants the loan realizes that after he leaves the banker's presence, other problems and matters may arise, and the banker may come out of the spell which he, the business man, has worked upon him through his good arguments and his presentation of facts. A business man in this situation always feels that if there was some way whereby he could hold the banker's mind in the same receptive and favorable condition that it was during the interview, there would be no question about a favorable decision a few hours or a few days later. The problem now is to keep the banker's mind impressed with the picture which the business man created there.

Or, take the example of a man or woman talking to a prospective buyer of a piece of property. The seller does his level best to create in the mind of the prospective buyer an excellent picture of the property and a favorable impression. The buyer decides to give his answer a few days later. The problem here, again, is to prevent the picture from fading out of the mind of the prospective buyer, and to keep the favorable impression constantly alive and vibrating.

Or, take the man or woman who interviews a prospective employer. After partially convincing the employer, the employee is told that a final decision will be made a few days later. Other applicants are to be interviewed. A confusion of pictures and facts will be built up in the employer's mind, and it will be difficult for him to recall clearly the next day the fine, definite picture which the applicant of today created in his mind.

The problem here is for the applicant to keep his impression in the mind of the employer until a decision is made.

How is one person to inhibit the mind of another so that the thoughts, ideas, pictures, facts, and impressions implanted in the mind will stay there, and keep revealing themselves like a motion picture to his consciousness, until he cannot eliminate them except by acting upon them and bringing the matter to a conclusion? All of you will agree with me that if there is a method for doing such a thing as this, it would be not only a legitimate thing to do, without violating any of the ethical laws of business, or the standards of the Cosmic principles, but it would also be an invaluable aid to all men and women.

Now crossing the fingers will do this very thing. I have found it to work in many cases, and I daily hear from those who have had it recommended to them by some acquaintance, and have found it successful in the first trial. Whatever faith you may put in the explanation I am going to give you, may or may not have a bearing upon its successful operation when you use it, but at least you may try it without jeopardizing any of your interests and without injury to your dignity and pride.

We know from psychological laws and principles, as well as from mystical practices, that the forefinger and second finger on each hand are the terminals of certain nerves which have to do with the centers of visualization in the mind, and the radiation of psychic waves in the process of telepathy. We know that these two fingers on each hand play an important part in so-called magnetic healing, or contact treatment work where the hands come in contact with the nerve centers of other bodies. We know that all through history these two fingers, with the addition of the thumb, have been used symbolically as the fingers from which there are potent radiations, often believed to be spiritual radiations, but now known to be magnetic, or of the nature of the mental essence.

A few years ago, an eminent scientist in Europe discovered that by pinching certain parts of the fingers, the outward flow of this same energy could be short-circuited for the relief of pain in various parts of the body. It was later found that all that was really done was to affect the mental activity of the consciousness. I could point out many other reasons to show that there is a relationship between the first and second finger of each hand, and the peculiar mental and psychic functions of the human mind. But in this talk I am not dealing with metaphysics or with other matters that are wholly within the realm of the scientific teachings of the Rosicrucian Order. I am dealing solely with the application of some principles to business affairs.

Now, according to the explanation that I have worked out, and which has been accepted by hundreds of persons who have delved deeply into the possibilities of this explanation, I am convinced that whenever we have mentally built up a definite picture or idea, thought or impression, which we are conveying to another mind, that a radiation can be created. As soon as we have completed the picture or impression in our mind and have expressed it to the mind of another, if we cross the forefinger and second finger of either hand or both hands, for a half hour or so, the impression thus created in the mind is caused to radiate in the form of telepathic waves from our mind to the mind of the person to whom we have just been speaking, and whose personality we associate with the impression we have in our minds.

I have found by test that if at certain hours during the day I think of the man that I interviewed yesterday, once more build up the pictures that I had presented to him in words, and then cross my fingers and hold that impression in my mind for ten minutes, that during those minutes the man once again recalls the impression I put into his mind, and thinks of me and the picture or story that I left with him. A great number of experiments of this kind were conducted by myself and others for the purpose of testing the principle involved, and, as I have said before, there are hundreds of business men who are using this method many times a day, and who do not hesitate to claim that the final results prove its efficiency. In many cases they have been able to ask the other fellow at just what hour or minute he had the recurring impressions, and they have found that these periods checked with the periods during which the fingers were crossed.

I remember one case very distinctly, which I think illustrates the whole principle involved. One afternoon, about 2:30, a man, who had been instructed in this process, rushed to a banker to present a proposition calling for a loan. He found that he could have only a three-minute interview with the president of the bank, for the president was about to step into his automobile, go to a railroad station, and take a train for a Northern city. He promised the client that he would decide the matter upon his return to the city three days later. The client returned to his office after the interview, and every half hour he sat in a relaxed condition, crossed his fingers for two minutes, and thought of the banker, while he built up again in his own mind the picture and story that he had given to the banker in words. That night, at eleven o'clock, the client received a telegram sent from a railroad station many miles distant, which read as follows: "Have thought of your proposition many times during afternoon and evening, and have decided to grant your request and am writing my bank accordingly." When the banker returned to the city, he was questioned by the client and admitted that he had sent the telegram in order to bring the matter to a conclusion. He wanted to get it out of his mind because he had been unable to think of any other matter during the afternoon and evening, and had to clear his mind of this recurring proposition in order to work out other problems pertaining to the matter which was taking him to a Northern city.

It may seem foolish to some of you to stop in the midst of your affairs many times a day, and in silence cross your fingers, and it may even seem like a waste of time. But if you had a big proposition pending, or an important matter hanging fire, you would not think it foolish if it was feasible to call the other fellow on the phone every half hour and remind him of your proposition. Such a method would probably annoy the other fellow and jeopardize your interests. Crossing your fingers has the advantage of diplomacy, for the other fellow may not be aware of your process, and it has the additional advantage of secrecy, for you can cross your fingers behind your back without revealing to anyone around you what you are doing, whereas telephoning is not always a private matter.

If you have followed all the suggestions I have given in my previous talks, you will undoubtedly find that crossing your fingers or keeping them crossed "just for luck" will prove to be one of the luckiest things you can do in bringing your affairs to a satisfactory conclusion.

Thus I make a plea for one form of superstition at least. And so far as I am personally concerned, I care little whether some practices are superstitious or not, so long as they work and produce results, and I have an explanation as to how they work that enables me to apply the process intelligently and understandingly. After all, that is as much as we can say about many things in life, and especially in connection with business and social affairs as we meet them in our commercial and home activities.

CHAPTER X

THE LAW OF COMPENSATION

AN HAS attempted in many ways to emulate or reduce to material form the Cosmic law of compensation; and while he has made a miserable failure of it in most ways, still, the spiritually-minded business man, or the mystical worker in the field of business, has succeeded in establishing in his own life and in the rules of his affairs, some principles which are truly representative of the Cosmic laws of compensation.

As I have said in preceding parts of this book, money as a means for rewarding and compensating men and women for their efforts is a false medium, and an arbitrary one, created by man without having the least relationship to the ideals of the Cosmic law.

It is fortunate, however, that while man on the one hand attempts to compensate those who serve him, and those who contribute to his needs by paying them money, the Cosmic law of compensation also operates to bring to each one of us a true compensation for what we have done. And in each element wherein man's method of compensation fails to reward or punish, adequately, for each good or evil deed, the Cosmic law properly, efficiently, and sufficiently compensates and makes full adjustment.

Man may scheme and plan to prevent the Cosmic law of compensation from operating in his individual case, and he may try to stay the great Cosmic laws from adequately adjusting the compensation for his acts. He may even succeed for a time in escaping what he believes is imminent, but it is a fact that no one has ever successfully avoided, evaded, or escaped the operation of the Cosmic law completely and continuously. Men and women may cheat one another of their just rewards, and men and institutes may fail wilfully or unconsciously to make proper compensation to men and women, but the Cosmic law never fails. It is immutable, of course, but it is also fair, just, and really worthy of our admiration when once we understand the principles of Cosmic compensation.

In business, the employer representing a great institution or a great corporation, or the employee representing himself as a mere human cog in the industrial machinery, must learn that injustice, unfair dealing, evil doing, and evil thinking will bring into operation the law of compensation as established in the Cosmic, and that there is no escape from the operation of this law. The employer or the employee who plans to take advantage of the faith, trust, and hope of another human being, or of a collection of human beings that represent a city, a nation or a continent, must expect the law of compensation to operate sooner or later, and bring punishment to the mind and interests of the person who planned the injustice.

It may be said that the law of compensation does not always bring an immediate manifestation of its operation, and that under the conditions in which we live man cannot always wait until the close of his life to enjoy the rewards of this Cosmic law, but must seek immediate rewards of a very definite nature each day and each week of his life. There is no warrant for the belief that the law of compensation defers its reward until the close of life. I believe this common misunderstanding is due to the preachments of certain religious doctrines that refer to the ultimate rewards that all good men and women will receive in the future state; but so far as the Cosmic law is concerned, it makes compensation adequately and properly in such ways and at such times as will render the most help and benefit to the deserving one.

With many business men and women with whom I have come in contact, the faith and trust in the operation of the law of compensation is equal to the faith or trust that many persons put into a superstition. Just as I have met rational business men who hesitate to pass under a ladder because of a conviction that within a few hours, or at the very next turn of their activities, some dire disaster would befall them, I have met many other men and women who believe most implicitly that whenever they do a kindness or an unselfish act for someone else or contribute in any way to the health and happiness of others, they can expect some reward or some Cosmic blessing, suddenly and uniquely, at almost the following hour. They had learned from experience that the Cosmic brings its rewards not only suddenly, but at a most propitious moment, and that by helping others or giving in whatever way they could to the needs and happiness of another, they were accruing a certain amount of Cosmic blessing or help that would come to them just when they needed it, and as they needed it.

I do not mean to say that such persons constantly had in mind the reward or return of their blessings whenever they planned to do something for someone else. I have noticed from many reports, and from intimate contact with those who followed such principles in their lives, that most of the unselfish or kindly acts performed by these persons were unplanned and wholly spontaneous, and that it was only as they were performing the act or immediately thereafter, that the thought came to them that in compensation for their rashness or liberality there would be the proper return. It is but natural for anyone promptly to question the logic of a spontaneous act or sudden urge, and to wonder whether it is worth while, diplomatic, or reasonable. It is at such moments of consideration of the spontaneous act that these persons generally conclude that even though it was sudden and probably urged by an emotional impulse, the Cosmic was conscious of the urge, and the whole-hearted response to it, and would compensate accordingly.

Let me illustrate how such cooperation with Cosmic law can really become a valuable asset in one's life. For a number of years I was closely associated with, and adviser to Mr. William Woodbury, who was one of New York's wealthy men given to the study of human needs. His business affairs with which I was connected were of such a nature as to permit him to have ample time for personal matters, and provided him with an income sufficient to allow him to indulge in any of the costly hobbies and practices which often become the ruination of many wealthy men. Mr. Woodbury, however, decided that he would get more pleasure out of life if he could evolve some plans of helping the worthy and needy who wanted to help themselves. He had no faith in organized charity, and did not believe that any form of charity helped the real man who had a real need.

Finally a plan was evolved whereby Mr. Woodbury set aside a million dollars in a bank in New York for the special purpose of helping others. He informed various business and charitable organizations that if they contacted any man, with a legitimate plan, who was anxious to go into business for himself, to send such a man to see him. Mr. Woodbury opened a special office in a private residence in a secluded part of New York City, and there, each morning, we interviewed applicants for help. Briefly outlined, his plan was to find such men as were competent in some definite line of business or trade, who had many years of experience in that particular line, and who were anxious to discontinue being employees and go into business for themselves. If such persons were well qualified in a moral and ethical way—that is, not addicted to drinking, gambling, or other extravagant indulgences—and were healthy and of an age which would permit the starting into business and the building up of a good following, he would loan them anywhere from five thousand to twenty-five thousand dollars, and in some cases even more. The money was loaned to such men without security, and with no other pledge or promise than their personal word, and with no agreement as to the return of the money except that it should be returned from the legitimate profits of their businesses, and in such payments as they found were possible, convenient, and not injurious to the progress of their business, and without any interest of any kind.

Within a year practically the whole of the million dollars had been loaned in this manner, and during the following year it was a pleasure to see that ninety-eight per cent of those who had secured the money were making various returns in accordance with the profits of their businesses, and in no wise attempting to defraud Mr. Woodbury. After four years of operation of the plan, Mr. Woodbury found that quite a few had returned not only the original amounts which they had borrowed, but had donated to the fund liberal amounts to help others, and that on the basis on which it was working, his original million dollars would be returned with a very much larger increase than if he had loaned it at six per cent. In fact, a report from Mr. Woodbury, to me, in

1924, showed that in ten years previous, his million dollars had been returned and a large additional fund accumulated; and he had proved his original contention that human nature could be trusted, and that the average man, if placed upon his word of honor, would not take advantage of any plan that was truly conceived to be non-commercial and one hundred per cent altruistic. Only a little over two per cent of the persons he had tried to help had taken advantage of the situation and had either absconded or in other ways defrauded him; but he took no means to punish them or even search for them.

The most important discovery made by Mr. Woodbury in connection with his humanitarian plan, however, was that soon after he inaugurated it his other business affairs began to prosper far beyond his anticipation, and many persons who owed him large sums of money began to make payments, and in other ways he found that the Cosmic law of compensation was beginning to reward him for his efforts in behalf of others. He finally organized an institution of helpfulness for business men, and up to the very last hour that it existed before being completely abandoned in order to carry on other activities, it was one of the outstanding demonstrations of Cosmic law. It is unfortunate that Mr. Woodbury is no longer in America to carry on these forms of help, but there are undoubtedly others in this country, and other countries, who have been doing and possibly are doing what Mr. Woodbury has done.

Another illustration is that of the work of Mr. Dodge, the New York financier, with whom I was associated as adviser and consultant in new plans for over five years. Mr. Dodge was not only well known throughout many Eastern cities as a promoter of big corporations and interested only in big business in every sense, but he was one of the most liberal workers, in behalf of the unfortunate men of the East, that I ever met. From one end of New York City to another Mr. Dodge was known in the principal hotels, restaurants, clothing stores, and real estate offices. When an unfortunate of either sex appeared at a restaurant or a hotel and asked for a room or a meal, and had a note written on the back of a card signed by Mr. Dodge, he or she was given every possible help.

And a note written by Mr. Dodge has given to many men and woman a receipt for a month's rent for their apartment or home, or some necessary furniture, groceries, or clothing.

It used to be a pleasure to go along with Mr. Dodge, in his automobile, once a month, to these principal stores, and listen to the reports, and note the pleasure Mr. Dodge had in handing out his personal checks to pay for the things others had received. What he had learned and what I knew of his business affairs, proved the soundness of his activities. There never was one of his big business propositions that did not pay and prove an eminent success. Whether in the Wall Street district, when several large financial institutions were amalgamated under his plan, or whether it was on the upper streets of Manhattan, when two large systems of chain drug stores were united into one of the largest drug corporations in the country under a plan outlined by him, or whatever it might have been, he seemed to have what others called "luck." And every person who had money for investment sought an opportunity to have an interest in any proposition that Mr. Dodge sanctioned or sponsored. He knew that he had Cosmic cooperation and support, because he believed himself to be one of the many silent and secret workers in behalf of the Cosmic to help his fellow men. It used to be a pleasure of his to tell a few others, quite confidentially, that he was incorporated, and that his firm consisted of the Cosmic Hosts and himself. With such a partnership, no man could fail in business.

Take the case of Sam Small, the president of the Board of Directors of one of the large cereal companies of America. Mr. Small was at one time an abandoned waif and had to fight his way through life, but he never forgot, in his days of wealth and prosperity, the suffering of the waifs of the street. It was indeed a pleasure for anyone to accompany him in his automobile several nights before Christmas each year, in whatever city he happened to be, and watch him go into the by-ways of congested districts among the poor, and pick up boys and girls and take them to clothing stores and buy them the shoes, stockings, and overcoats which they needed, and send them home with baskets of groceries or buy them toys. Hun-

dreds of them in many cities were helped in this
manner, each Christmas, without ostentation, and
with no other motive than the soul pleasure he
derived from it, and the idea that some divine law
had raised him from poverty as a waif to great
wealth for the purpose of enabling him to carry
out the Cosmic principles. He could not conceive
of the possibility of his wealth having come to him
for his own selfish use or the use of his immediate
family exclusively, and he had the true idea of
being a steward of divine funds. And yet as fast
as Mr. Small expended his funds in this manner,
his income was increased and increased until he
finally became the head of many big companies.

Mr. Small and many others would frankly tell
you that at times, when they first felt the urge to
give to others and to help others, they often had
to debate whether the few dollars they possessed
should be rashly or spontaneously divided and
given away, or held in reserve for a possible rainy
day. Many times the money in hand represented
just a safe margin for emergencies in their business
affairs, and in some cases the plan for helpfulness
called for the expenditure of every available dollar,

and the jeopardizing of personal interests at the time. Yet there was always the conviction, based upon previous experience, that if even the last penny is given away freely and without reluctance, and with that spontaneity of good will that the Cosmic always uses, there would come a proper reward in the form of some adjustment of financial affairs that would remove any possibility of disastrous results to the giver.

And so my plea to you must be, that regardless of the station in life you occupy, or the situation of your business and financial affairs, you must not permit your own needs, and especially your contemplated needs, to interfere with the liberality of your charity or the broadness of your helpfulness. It is a positive fact, that as you act spontaneously and freely, and without hesitation or long deliberation, in the giving to someone else of that which you can give but which you could use yourself, so you will find the Cosmic spontaneously and liberally coming to your aid at the proper time, and with the same lack of hesitancy which you manifested.

It is safe to say that the average person of health and business capabilities who finds himself or herself out of employment, out of funds, and out of contact with any who can help or tide over the serious situation, is a person who has failed in the past to give liberally and spontaneously when the Cosmic urge came from within. Too many persons appeal to the Cosmic or to the laws of psychology and mysticism for aid in their predicaments, who cannot show that at any time in the past have they cooperated with the Cosmic in liberally helping others. Merely to give advice to others who seek it, or simply to give a meal to one who begs at the door, or to drop a few coins in the Salvation Army pot, or to donate some old clothing to the orphan asylum is not carrying out the greater work of the Cosmic. Those who suddenly feel that there is something they can do for someone, something they can give, even though it hurts in a financial or material way, or something that they can do even though it is inconvenient, unpleasant, tiresome, and costly, and without hesitation, without reluctance, whole-heartedly submit to the urge, are the ones who are truly cooperating with the Cosmic, and find eventually, not in the days of the last judgment in the world beyond, but in the days here and now, that at every crisis and in every need the Cosmic comes to their aid abundantly.

It behooves everyone, therefore, who has read this book through with the hope of finding in it some help in the solving of his personal problems, to ask himself this question: "What have I done for others?" And perhaps this additional question: "What have I contributed to the Cosmic supply that I may now appeal to its teller and withdraw from the positive supply?" If you can find no positive affirmative answer to your questions, and you believe, even half reluctantly, that you have been deficient in your cooperation with the Cosmic in this regard, it will be well for you to consider immediately how you may proceed at once to help some others while you are seeking help for yourself. Before you expect any return through Cosmic or mystic laws, be sure that you have done your utmost to help someone else, not only because of the reward that will come to you, but because it is your duty, as it is the duty of every human being, to be an earthly instrument in the carrying out of the Cosmic scheme of things.

For the Home and Business

And as long as you are out of attunement with the Cosmic plans, and not a part of the army of Cosmic workers, you cannot expect the Cosmic laws to help you and be unmindful of your neglect.

Perhaps your very situation today, in whole or in part, and perhaps the problems which you now face, and from which you have sought relief or now seek relief, is a result of your failure to co-operate with the law of compensation in the past, and, therefore, your present predicament is a part of your Karma. If this is so—and no one else but you can tell that—it is certain that you must adjust the conditions first with the Cosmic law, and with the Cosmic Hosts, and then with man on earth.

CHAPTER XI

ATTRACTING PATRONAGE

NE OF THE most common complaints voiced in letters to our various welfare departments is to the effect that keen competition or rivalry is responsible for the troubles and poor progress in the line of business owned or operated by the writers. In other words, the writers of such letters say: "I was getting along all right with my business, which was slowly building up and becoming profitable, but others near me have entered into the same line of business and the patronage is now divided between a number and none of us are succeeding as well as we should." Other letters say: "A competitor has entered my field of business and is near me, drawing so heavily upon my patronage that my business is about to fail. I am honest, give proper returns for the money, and have tried to build my business on a fair and square basis; yet I now face failure because of this competition."

It is absolutely true that competition is the spice of business and that keen competition should result in keener business for the keen business man. There is hardly any business today that does not have competition, and if it has no competition, it soon will have; and everyone who is in business whether for himself or for another, should realize that competition is no explanation of failure, but should be a real incentive for success.

I remember the story of a clergyman who came to me and told me that the attendance at his Sunday evening and Wednesday evening service was being ruined by lack of patronage because a motion-picture theatre across the street was attracting everyone in the town and drawing from his congregations. I asked him if it was hurting his Monday night, Tuesday night, Thursday night, Friday night, and Saturday night congregations, and he told me that he had none on those nights, for his church was closed on all those evenings. I asked him to describe the front of his church so that I might get a picture of what the church looked like. He went into detail whereby I was able to visualize one of those nice gray stone structures often seen in the heart of some middle-sized town, with ivy growing over the doorway and around the windows, an old belfry with rusty, dusty bells, a little lawn in front of the church, badly kept, and huge, wooden doors in the doorway, closed and securely locked. The structure I saw in my mind could have been a suitable place for a prison, an insane asylum, a sanitarium, or the winter home of an erratic old man of wealth. I asked him if he had any signs or emblems on the front of the church and he said there was a cross on the top of the belfry that was once gilded but now quite rusted, and two signs on the front of the building, one on either side of the door. When I asked what the signs said, he answered:

"The sign on the left side of the door is small, with a black background and gold lettering which says that the Reverend John Blank, D.D., is Pastor, and that services are held Sundays at eleven o'clock, three o'clock, and seven-thirty, and on Wednesday nights at seven-thirty, and that *all are welcome.* The sign on the right-hand side of the door is black, with gold lettering, and states that John Sexton is the undertaker and sexton."

Then I asked the clergyman: "What kind of a building does the motion-picture concern have?" He explained to me that it had a white and green tiled archway with a large, well-decorated lobby, an attractive ticket booth, many lights, and attractive signs, and was in full operation every night in the week. Then I asked him to step with me mentally into the middle of the street on any evening at about seven-thirty and consider the mental attitude of a person who had an evening to spare and was trying to decide where to go. On the one side of the street was the church, and on the other side the motion-picture theatre. The one structure is dark, gruesome-looking, uninviting. No strains of music come from within, no face appears at the door to greet you, and the only signs that you can read, politely tell you that the place is open on only a few occasions during the week, and that two persons are connected with it—one who is ready to tell you how sinful you are and the other will bury you when you die. On the other side of the street there is warmth, color, attractiveness, gaiety, interesting music, and a smiling face at a booth inviting you to come in, and the signs in front of this place tell you that a number of characters will appear before you to speak to you or portray stories and lessons, and that these stories and lessons deal with the realities of life, the actual occurrences, the things of *here* and *now*, and bespeak generally the land of the living and the life of happiness and joy.

Of course the clergyman could see the point of my discussion with him. Instead of complaining and attempting to discover all the wrong things he could find about the motion-picture theatres and the motion-picture industry generally, he should have analyzed his own situation and tried to find what was wrong with him and his church. Man is unquestionably religiously inclined, and the average man and woman would be the last one to think of having the church left out of community life. But the average man and woman want a religion that is *joyous* and *inspiring* and filled with hope and salvation that is a saving grace from all the trials, troubles, sorrows, and tribulations of this life. The church, as conducted by this particular clergyman, was an institution of sadness and despondency. His own record showed that he was catering more to elderly people than to younger people, and that in fact he could not get any of the young people to any of the evening services.

I found a year later, after this man had kept his church open seven nights a week and had arranged interesting and instructive programs for each night, that he was operating a keen form of competition to the theatre, for the folks in the town found that they could get cleaner entertainment and more real benefit out of some of the week-day church services than they got at the motion-picture theatre, and at a smaller price. Since it was not a matter of *price competition* but of *audience*, the clergyman had the upper hand all the time, but did not know it.

Speaking of theatres, I remember an early experience with a neighborhood motion-picture theatre in the residential section of the upper part of New York. A number of men who had never been in the motion-picture business but who had some ideas to test in regard to how a theatre should be conducted, pooled their funds and turned a small store building into a very attractive motion-picture theatre. The theatre seated only three hundred persons, and in those days a neighborhood theatre did not dare to charge more than fifteen cents for a seat. They believed they could get twenty-five cents if there was a good show, and if the theatre was properly conducted. If the house was filled every evening at its two performances, the total income for the night would be one hundred and fifty dollars. That amount of money would not go far in putting on first run pictures and having some good vaudeville acts and good music. Therefore, elaborate programs and costly features had to be eliminated, and what was used had to be presented in a unique manner in order to appeal. After everything was done to make the entrance and the interior of the theatre attractive in an artistic way, even to having some mural artists make some very unusual paintings on the walls and in the lobby, and after an attractive stage with various beautiful scenic drops had been completed, the theatre was ready for its opening.

In order to fight the competition of the large downtown theatres, not more than five minutes' ride from this neighborhood, the owners of this theatre consulted with me in regard to a plan of solicitation whereby an appeal could be made for patronage among the well-to-do and the cultured who would make this their private or personal amusement house. Letters were sent to the Board of Education and to the schools in the neighborhood, announcing the opening of the theatre and stating that the theatre would not be open on school afternoons so as not to tempt the youths to stay away from school; that children would not be permitted in the evenings without their parents; and that only clean and wholesome pictures, free from rowdyism or crime, would be shown. This announcement made a "hit" with the teachers and the Board of Education, and with the churches and the better families of the neighborhood. Then an engraved invitation was sent to every well-to-do family within a mile of the theatre, announcing the opening of the *Venetian Theatre* with its Italian orchestra, Italian decorations, Italian atmosphere, and Italian courtesy. We assured them that they would find a better program, more comfortable seats, a more wholesome environment, and more courtesy than they had ever found in any theatre before. They were invited to come to the opening night free by using the ticket that was enclosed.

The theatre was packed on its first night, and in the three years that it continued it was packed every night at each performance. When the patrons came to the door they were ushered politely and with real courtesy to their seats. Every convenience was provided, even to the extent of having the seats wider and further apart than they were in ordinary theatres. For the first time in the history of any New York theatre, drinking water was freely distributed in sanitary cups between the various acts. As patrons left they were handed a little card thanking them for their patronage and inviting them to come again and make this theatre their evening home of pleasure.

The courtesies and attentions did not extend solely to the patrons, but to the vaudeville performers and everyone acting as an employee. After it had been in operation for three months, I went to the dressing rooms behind the stage and found that even individual bathrooms had been built in the corner of each dressing room, and that a shower-bath and a little kitchenette for the preparation of hurried meals had been provided for the performers. I found notations written on the white walls of the dressing rooms stating that the undersigned couple, or individual performer, wanted to say that he or she had never been in any other theatre where such courtesies were practiced. They wished the theatre well and expressed enjoyment in performing in it. In the downtown booking office where the vaudeville acts were engaged, the men praised the system that the theatre used and sent only the cleanest and best acts it had. Before the theatre was a year old, it had forced out of business a number of cheap ten-and-fifteen-cent motion-picture houses within two or three blocks of this new place.

Here was the art of attracting patronage brought to a high degree, and proved to be the proper way in which to build business in the face of competition.

Even those theatres that were forced to go out of business could have saved themselves by immediately adopting the same policy that the *Venetian Theatre* used. They claimed that the *Venetian Theatre* had made a tremendous investment in decorations, musicians, uniforms for ushers, and other incidentals that they could not afford. The truth of the matter was that the biggest investment that the *Venetian Theatre* made was an investment in *politeness* and *unique business methods* that did not cost anything but some thought and considerable sincerity.

The business man who says that he is giving full measure for every dollar received, and, therefore, is entitled to patronage, is fooling himself. It is only natural for the average man and woman to expect full value *plus* for every dollar he or she spends, and the *plus* part of the return does not have to be in material form. There was a time when thirteen doughnuts constituted a dozen in the bakery shop, and the extra doughnut was supposed to be a bid for patronage. So much did the average bakery shop count on the extra doughnut or the extra roll in each dozen that they almost threw the bag at you, grabbed your money, and let you go. They expected the prize doughnut or roll to sweep you off your feet and paralyze you into believing that you simply had to go to that particular bakery or do without.

Now, any live bakery could have gotten away with eleven doughnuts for a dozen, if in place of the other doughnuts it had handed out a good *big handful of politeness, courtesy,* and a little touch of *unique service.* I saw this proved in a bakery that opened its doors against keen competition. It did not give the extra doughnut in each dozen, but it did use a unique bag for its doughnuts that did not get greasy and become a telltale article in the hands of every woman who carried the bag around with her during the rest of her shopping; and it sold more warm biscuits every afternoon than any of the other bakeries because it did not wait for its customers to come to the store counters and ask for them, but sent them around to every home promptly at four o'clock every afternoon in unique little boxes. They collected for them at the end of the week. Who could resist warm tea biscuits at four o'clock in the afternoon?

I know of a men's furnishing store that opened in the face of keen competition and walked away with all of the neighborhood business in a few months by adding some unique features. For instance, it did not sell neckties by hanging them on racks or by displaying them in a glass case. The store had a little booth conveniently situated with a bright light in it and a chair and a mirror where a prospective customer of neckties could sit down and try on one or a dozen and see how they actually looked when tied in his collar or around his neck. Women hold dresses up to their faces to see how the color agrees with their complexion, or at least all sensible women do this. Very few men have any idea how a necktie will look when it is off the rack and close to their chin, and a tie that looks nicely tied in a knot held by the salesman, looks like *anything else* when it is around the neck of the man who wants to buy it. They soon found that men also tried on collars in this same way, and their collar business increased along with the necktie business. The man who owned the store believed that if you tried on shoes, and tried on suits, to see if they fit you, you should also try on neckties and collars. The little loss through wrinkled neckties and an occasional soiled collar was more than offset by the tremendous business he did.

Many lines of business are failing today, or falling into the hands of incompetent, irresponsible persons because men who have money to invest believe that some of these lines of business are failures, and cannot be put on a high plane. The average man with several thousand dollars to invest who wants to enter a dignified business thinks that conducting a garage is one of the lowest, meanest, or dirtiest jobs that he can have. Some men believe that such a thing as a garage should be left for mechanics or persons incapable of conducting any other kind of business. The result is that the average garage and repair shop for automobiles is an uninviting and irresponsible institution. For this reason patrons do not want to pay well, are always suspicious about the charges asked, and take with a grain of salt any statements as to the efficiency of the work performed. The result is that a garage in any community is like a prophet in his own country. The people who live near it or closest to it will not patronize it, but go into other fields where the grass seems greener or conditions seem better.

For the Home and Business

There is no reason in the world why a garage business and repair shop could not be established and maintained in a high-class manner without any more investment or any more operating costs than is required by an ordinary garage. Why it is not done more often is an indication of the inability of men to think along unique lines and to create a new aspect and a new character for the business they are in.

There is no surer way of attracting patronage than by making the new customer or the old customer feel that from the moment he crosses the threshold of your doorway he is in a different place and going to receive different attention and different service than he has received before. When a customer feels that some distinct service and some special courtesy, that he has not asked for and is not expected to pay for, is going to be given to him, or is *being given* to him, he begins to make a mental note of the place and decides that if everything turns out well, he will come again. And when a customer can walk out of your place of business saying to himself that regardless of what he paid, or what he received, he also received what he did not pay for, and what he did not expect, and what he did not find anywhere else, then you will have a patron who will stay with you as long as you can keep him thinking that way.

There is a big difference between politeness and sycophancy, and between courtesy and servility. No customer wants to be filled with large slices of the delicatessen article that is so popular nowadays as a symbol of flattery, and which no matter how thinly it may be sliced, still retains its nature in the mind of every intelligent person. On the other hand, there is a way to extend courtesy and demonstrate politeness that will leave its impression long after the demonstrator of these things has forgotten it.

No matter what business you may be in, or for whom you may be working, you will better the interests of the firm, and incidentally yourself, if you try to give every customer, every patron, every client, *more* than he pays for, and remember again that the "more" need not refer to the material things being sold. A railroad company is not in business to sell tickets. It is a service company, and unless service is given along with the ticket, and carried out by the ticket and the sellers of the ticket, the company is not giving its patrons what it is in business to give. The ticket is but the symbol of what is to follow. The customer does not buy a railroad ticket for one hundred dollars in order to have a nice, green piece of paper in his wallet. It is what the ticket represents that he pays his money for and by which he judges the efficiency of the company. You could not make patrons continue to use any particular railroad because of an attempt to make them fall in love with the color scheme of the prettily engraved ticket you sell them.

The service that goes along with the selling of a suit of clothes, and continues long after the man has been wearing the suit, will bring that man back into the store again, when the *high quality* of the merchandise for which he paid *adequately* would make no impression upon him. When you sell a man an ice-cream soda, you cannot argue with him that you are giving him his money's worth of *water, gas* and *frozen cream*. It is the cleverness of the mixture, the uniqueness of the service, the comfort in enjoying it, and the environment of the whole occasion, that makes the hit with the thirsty man or woman.

Therefore, in attracting patronage remember that you must use subtle and psychological principles and put them into such outward manifestation that the person to be affected realizes them keenly, and makes a mental note of them. The process is entirely up to you and not up to the customer. If your competitors are taking your business away from you or from the employer who employs you, it is up to the employer *and you* to win the customers back, provided the merchandise is good and the business is an honest one. If your competitors are beating you in the game of giving *plus* in every deal, you have got to go one better with them and add *plus* to *plus*. It is not a matter of the survival of the fittest, but a survival of the *best giver;* and again I say, the things that count most with the customer, client, or patron in any line of business are the things *he did not pay for,* did not expect, and which do not have any material price attached to them.

Chapter XII

THE SKELETON IN THE CLOSET

E MAY dodge the issue as we please and try to convince ourselves that the idea is only theoretical and not a scientific fact, but the truth remains, nevertheless—all our problems of health and personal affairs have a cause within ourselves.

Only recently, an eminent medical authority speaking before a large congregation of physicians and surgeons said that his experience of a quarter of a century as a physician, surgeon, author, and professor in a medical school had convinced him that after the physician had completed his diagnosis of the symptoms and had made a careful examination into the pathological and histological causes of the ill-health of a person, there was still a very large and more important field for investigation. The field was the inner self of the patient. He claimed that until the physician knew as much about the personal, private thinking, and acting of the patient in his dealings with all human affairs, the physician could not know the real cause of a mental or physical disturbance.

The psychoanalyst and the psychiatrist long ago learned to seek beyond the outer self for the cause of many peculiar mental and physical traits. The real mystic knows that what a person thinks, believes, talks about, and does in his daily affairs, has as much effect upon his health and personal problems as have contaminated foods, disease germs in the air, unhygienic environments, accidents to the body, and stock market fluctuations.

After twenty-five years of watching the systematic and carefully recorded activities of the Council of Solace of the Rosicrucian Order in America, I have become thoroughly convinced of the universal truth and principle revealed in my personal experiences with persons whom I have helped in many problems. To sum this up, I would say that I have found it is absolutely futile and a waste of time to attempt metaphysically or psychically, as well as medicinally or legally, to help a person who is sick or in business trouble if such a person continues to do, think, and believe the false, erroneous, or inharmonious things which are the real causes of his trouble.

Let me cite one case that will probably reveal this idea to you clearly and quickly. A man came to me who had been suffering from boils and carbuncles for a little over two years. When he came to my office on the recommendation of an eminent physician, I was horrified at the painful and obnoxious appearance of his countenance through the presence of two large boils on either cheek. The back of his neck and even part of the scalp where the hair had been shaved was scarred from previous lance incisions for the removal of boils and carbuncles, and he told me he had had them on various parts of his body. His doctor verified the fact that he and other physicians had used everything known to the medical science to clarify and purify the man's blood, and there was no question about the fact that the impurities which accumulated in each carbuncle or boil came from impurities in his blood. His blood seemed to be continuously poisoned with a form of poison that insisted on breaking out in a horrible manner. Medical science had done its utmost to cleanse his blood and body in a chemical, physiological sense. Even his food for the past six months had been carefully regulated, cleansed, and all water boiled. He was not engaged in any business that would bring him in contact with poisons of any kind. The boils were increasing in number and size. The history of his case clearly showed that each month brought more and larger amounts of poison and pus into manifestation.

I noticed that in addition to the man's suffering from pain, he was very curt, brusque, and inclined to be impatient. I discounted the other attitude of his mind which was caused by his complete skepticism and doubt about any psychologist or mentalist doing anything for him. This attitude, however, did reveal the fact that he had no faith in any religious principles relating to the power or advantage of mental culture and right thinking. I talked with the man on various subjects, always ignoring his impatience with what he probably considered my foolish belief in spiritual things, and then sent him on his way while I made an investigation of the psychic impression I received from him. I found that the man was not only a critic of the church and refused even to have a Bible in his home, but more important than this, he was a typical "bully" in his home, in his social circles, and in the business place where he worked. He had, among other superb mental attributes, a most horrible temper, and his associates where he worked said it was common for him to have an outburst of temper at least once a day, and during these fits, which were often provoked by the mere dropping of a tool or instrument, or the finding of something misplaced by him, he would slam things from the bench where he worked, kick the boxes and barrels or machinery near him even to such an extent that he often harmed his own person. He had been known to smash his hand through the plate glass of a window because it refused to close for him, and thereby cut his hand badly. Another time, he kicked at a piece of iron that was in his way and injured his toe. He had often pulled his hair so ferociously that he had made his scalp bleed.

The man became a beast or a brute without any control of himself when suddenly annoyed over some simple little thing. In his home, his wife and children were afraid to cross him in any remark or to contradict or correct him in any misstatement. He had been known to upset the entire dining-room table, causing all the dishes and food to be thrown onto the floor, merely because of his displeasure at some dish of food. In the corner cigar store where he spent an occasional hour gossiping with some men, he was called "the agitator" and was annoying and unpleasant to everyone. He was firmly convinced that all politicians were crooked, that the government was being run for the advantage of the rich and the suffering of the poor. He was also convinced that the churches were built for no other purpose than to ring their bells on Sunday morning when he wanted to sleep, and silver dollars were made by the government only to wear holes in his pocket.

Nothing in the world was just right, not even himself, for he admitted that he could not live as properly and happily as he should because nothing afforded him the opportunity and that he would be better off in his grave than alive. If ever there was a human piece of machinery manufacturing virulent poison for self-consumption, it was this specimen of humanity. Between sunrise and sunset of each day, he created more actual poison in his blood stream than would be found in an army of soldiers fighting at the front with all of their hatred or supposed hatred toward the enemy.

When all of this was explained to his physician, he agreed that this mental attitude of the man *might* be responsible for the boils. Naturally, he was reluctant to concede that he had overlooked this condition in his diagnosis. However, knowing the possible cause did not tell us how we were going to correct it. It was unthinkable that we could accomplish anything by telling the man about his faults and asking him to change them. Even our suggestion of such a thing to him would have resulted in another outburst of temper and the creation of another ounce of poison. Most certainly, his wife or children would not dare to venture such a suggestion. We finally secured the cooperation of his employer in the interests of medical research. The man was transferred to an experimental station in the country operated by the concern he was working for. The concern was making a new model for home lighting and power equipment. The man was sent to a farm in Pennsylvania, eighteen miles from the nearest small city. For four months he had to live among peaceful, quiet, retiring farmers, and do nothing but watch the operation and general results of a small light and power plant temporarily installed in an empty barn. There was nobody he could quarrel with because all had been warned in advance not to get into any arguments with him, but to look upon him as a scientist who should be left alone with his thoughts undisturbed. There was little opportunity for impolite or even polite criticism of food or conditions around him. After two months, his boils began to lessen and his blood cleared up considerably, for the physician who had been treating him for a number of months made it his business to go to Pennsylvania and call on him. In six months he returned to New York in a very clean condition.

To prove that it was neither the climate nor the food, nor the water that affected his blood, he was given charge of a small experimental shop in the Bronx where the new model of the power equipment was being secretly perfected. He had only one young man as an assistant and it was arranged that he should sleep at the plant as watchman at night with an extra fee for this special service. Therefore, he ate all of his meals at various restaurants and could pick the menus to suit himself. He quarreled little with the young man and his outbursts of temper were seldom. His blood remained in a fairly good state and no boils appeared for another six months. Then he was brought back to his old environment again, and although he had been partly cured of his habit of a daily outburst of temper, he had many of them each month through his arguments with employees and arguments at home, and in the cigar store, and in six months he again had a few more boils. All of us who were interested in the experiment were thoroughly convinced that he himself mentally and physically caused the poison in his system.

This is an extreme case, of course, but while this man may have created an ounce of poison in his system every day, there are millions of men and women who are creating a grain of poison of some kind in their systems every week, and it does not take much of this mental and spiritual, or psychic poison to accumulate and become responsible for many mental and physical ills as well as business difficulties and personal problems. I have known of persons whose health continued to be below par solely because they held continuously in the secret parts of their natures a life-long grudge against another person, the mention of whose name would always cause an uprising of the inner spirit in the form of hatred and evil thoughts, even though not a word was expressed. I have known of those who suffered from headaches, depressed emotions, and slight forms of dizziness, solely because of an attitude of envy, dislike, distrust, jealousy, or some other unkind thought or feeling toward some persons, groups of persons, or conditions.

In business and personal problems, I have found the same thing to be true: The owner of a store, the owner of a manufacturing business, the salesman, the clerk, or anyone else engaged in business who goes about his daily affairs with an inharmonious although secret attitude toward some person, group of persons, business associates, or business conditions, generally is sure to have trouble and experience a definite form of reflection of his mental attitude. His business will decrease, he will find competitors succeeding while he fails, or he will find good opportunities passing him by and favoritism and patronage ignoring him.

Usually it is very difficult for the person thus suffering to analyze just what it is he is thinking or believing, or inwardly expressing, that is the real cause of his troubles. The average person seems to think that a personal enmity of a passive or private nature toward some other individual is an inconsequential thing as long as he or she does not go about expressing it or allowing it to come into outer manifestation. That is a mistake. The poison is in the system just the same, whether expressed by violent outbursts of temper, in an occasional unkind word or remark, or privately held confidential.

There is hardly a patient that our Council of Solace contacts psychically or mentally that does not register some long well-established prejudice, ill feeling, erroneous thought, or unkind sentiment lurking in the system like a germ sapping the vitality of health and causing an inharmonious relationship with Cosmic laws and principles. Such persons can be neither healthy, happy, nor prosperous in any of the affairs of life until they are purged of this subtle, secret, private influence within their beings. After all, there is no one better able to analyze these things and discover the germ within the psychic system than the patient himself, if he would be but honest and truthful, fair, and just in his self-examination.

Therefore, whatever may be the problem confronting you in life, whether it be ill-health, a mild mental condition that is annoying, a lack of ability or power to attract success and happiness, or a continuous failure of your plans or desires, look within yourself for some subtle, mental cause, not necessarily related in any way to your health or your personal problems, but most surely related to the harmonious relationship that should exist between you and all living beings and the universe generally. Seek for the skeleton in your closet. This is far more important than any skeletons in the old family closet that you feel you may have inherited, or any skeletons of germs and bugs that may be in your food or drink, or in the air you breathe. Get that skeleton out of your closet, dust it off, and have a good look at it, and see what a tricky, satanic creature it really is, and how unworthy it is to be a part of yourself, and hide within the sacred precincts of your temple. Then, after having paid homage to its subtle powers, inter it in the earth of oblivion and erect a tombstone over it with the words, "Here 'lies' an untruth." Then ask the God of your heart and the Masters of the Cosmic realms to keep you clean and holy and undefiled in your thoughts and in your attitude toward all beings. By cleansing the inside of the cup, your drinks of life will not be poisoned. No other Cosmic principle, metaphysical law, or material help will bring you one iota of benefit until you are right with the Cosmic and attuned to the harmony of the universe and love your neighbor and all creatures as you love yourself.

T WOULD appear from a careful survey of the success attained by a large majority of the Rosicrucians who have used the unique principles to improve their health and enlarge their social and financial standings, that these persons have used freely such methods, principles, processes, and formulas as might be used by every man and woman without limiting themselves to the exclusion of any principle or idea that was sane and sensible.

In other words, it is found in the review of the lives of most of the highly successful Rosicrucians that no element of fanaticism and no degree of bigotry or narrowness has entered into their application of Nature's laws and power. Just because one man finds in the Rosicrucian teachings some principles that are unique and efficient and worthy of continuous application, there is no reason to reject from one's mode of living and from one's scheme for advancement any principle or idea that is *good,* and yet not essentially *Rosicrucian.* In this we see the broadness of the Rosicrucian idea, and it illustrates the working out of the thought constantly presented to Rosicrucians; namely, that one must be, above all else, sane, reasonable, and broad-minded.

The true Rosicrucian comes to know very early in his experiments with the teachings that the doctrines of the Rosicrucians are not intended to be a limited creed or an exclusive outline of the only laws and principles of value to man in his personal evolution. As inclusive as the teachings have been made and are being made, the fact remains that man is constantly discovering or evolving methods and processes for his own advancement which may not be found in the Rosicrucian teachings or in the teachings of any other school or system. Some schools or movements insist that in order that success with their work may be attained, the student or the practitioner must exclude everything that is not a part of their systems.

We find physicians of some schools of medicine who are so old-fashioned in their beliefs and comprehension of the newer laws that they insist that the patient must not accept or receive any other form of help for his physical disability than that being prescribed by him in accordance with the indications of his system. On the other hand, we find the broad-minded and more modern physician freely admitting that in addition to the medicine, surgery, or adjustments prescribed by him, the patient may have the benefit also of metaphysical, mental, or psychological treatments. Such physicians are not only helping their patients to attain normality in a more rapid manner, but they are establishing faith and confidence in the minds of their patients by showing a tolerant attitude, and an understanding of the possibilities of various laws to affect certain conditions.

The Rosicrucians freely proclaim and demonstrate that the mind of man is capable of many marvelous controls over the physical body, and that through psychological or psychic and mental principles man may alleviate pain and suffering and produce many cures. On the other hand, Rosicrucianism plainly and distinctly indicates that where medicine or herb extracts, surgery or me-

chanical adjustments, massage or electricity, tooth
extraction, eye correction, or any other improvement in the physical, chemical, anatomical, or
functional condition of the body is indicated, these
things should be attended to immediately and at
the hands of a competent person, thoroughly
trained in a college devoted to that work and
licensed to practice his art or science. To believe
that psychological principles will take the place of
these other processes or methods is simply to shut
the door to efficient aid and depend upon faith or
the operation of natural law to effect a gradual
change, or permit a temporary condition to become a chronic one and thereby more serious than
it was.

The same thing may be said of business ills, social ills, and the general ills of humanity. Miracles
are performed by the mind and also by the hand,
and many of the great miracles of the past that are
recorded in sacred literature as having been made
manifest through prayer or the application of a
divine Principle are being duplicated today by
science through a more direct application of natural laws. The manifest miracle is the same in

both cases, and where science or the arts and laws of the natural world will competently and efficiently adjust matters for man, he is extremely foolish to ignore these other methods and depend solely upon faith or his finite understanding of infinite principles.

To be highly successful in life, men and women must cease believing or feeling that they are individuals, independent of all other persons or beings in the universe. It is only through a developed sense of oneness with God and oneness with mankind that man attunes himself rightfully to the conditions that surround him, and which will carry him onward to success, happiness, and health, if he masters the obstacles that seem to rise before him. Most of the obstacles in life which men and women look upon as mountainous barriers to the goal of life are fictitious things, and often figments of the imagination or phantasmagories of the fear element that still resides in the minds of men and women as an inheritance from the primitive stages of existence.

One old mystic said that the things we feared the most in life were the things that never happened; and I know from personal and correspondence contact with thousands of men and women, who write to the Council of Solace of the Rosicrucians for aid and help in overcoming the obstacles that they believe stand before them, that the statement of this old mystic is true. There is a trite saying that one should never cross a bridge until one comes to it, and I have found that the average man or woman who hesitates in venturing along the path to success is not only trying to cross a bridge that is far in the distance, but is making of that bridge a greater structure and a greater test of endurance than is warranted by the actual facts. In fact, many of them are not sure that there is a bridge to be crossed, but on the basis that no long road continues in any direction without going over some bridges, they anticipate the existence of them in their lives and proceed to worry about the crossing.

After all, the road to success is like unto the road to happiness, prosperity, health, or pleasure. It is not likely to be entirely level, always straight, not always free from showers, storms, or muddy spots, or even rocky beds. But these little difficulties or inconveniences are part of the game of life, and the one who is deterred or discouraged by these conditions when he approaches them is the one who fails to make the goal. But as I have intimated, there are many who permit themselves to be deterred on the path while it is still level, smooth, straight, and convenient, because of an anticipation of some incline, some curve, or some unpleasant condition.

Man has been given more faculties and more marvelous abilities to direct and control his life than any other of the living creatures of this earth. He possesses the ability to reason and reach conclusions and establish through his will power a determination to carry out his conclusions against obstacles and conditions which deter other creatures and hold them within limits unknown to man. The strongest of the creatures of less intelligence than man are easily held within bounds by means and methods that the average man would smile at as a barrier to his freedom. The wildest and strongest lion of Africa, though demonstrating its prowess in many ways, is easily held within a limited area by an iron grating or a wall that would mean nothing to a man who was determined to pass beyond such an interference to his freedom. We know that men who have been confined within prison walls have pitted their ingenuity, strength, and endurance against the minds of the most skillful engineers and architects in escaping from such limitations. If the same amount of thought and determination were used by the average man in attempting to overcome the obstacles that beset him in his attempt to succeed in life, with all of the freedom of thought and action that is natural to the average man, he would make a greater success of his life.

Man has within him a creative power that is a part of the universal creative force and is a part of the creative energy which God breathed into space when the first Word was spoken, and order came out of chaos. Science is constantly proving, and the psychic powers within man are constantly demonstrating, that there is no limit to the possibilities of this creative power. Man has yet to discover in any of the fields of science, or in the domain of psychology and metaphysics, the limit of that creative power when it is focused upon some issue or upon some condition.

Much has been said in recent years about the *death ray,* or that invisible beam of light that may be focused upon living matter and through its high frequency or high rates of vibrations bring a cessation of vibratory animation and produce so-called *death.* The vibrations of this beam are not potentially destructive, but creative, and it is because of their high creative potentiality that they disturb the equilibrium or harmonium of living cells and bring about a change of expression. That change may bring "death" to the form of expression upon which the vibrations are directed, but will bring new life into the newer forms of expression that result therefrom. The power of this invisible beam, and the greatest amount of energy that may be put back of it at the hands of science, cannot possibly equal in strength the creative power that man may focus upon an issue or condition, and, in this wise, affect things in his life which this marvelous beam could not affect at all.

The Divinity in man is the only real part of his existence, and all else is but a servant unto it.

The world is the footstool for this Divine Being, and everything in the universe is enslaved by the omnipotent intelligence of this highest expression of creation. This Divine Self of man knows neither disease nor death, failure, nor discouragement. Its trend of activity is always upward and progressive. Its outlook is altruistic, optimistic, and joyful. Its intellectual resources are unlimited. Its capabilities are as wide as the universe itself. It is only the outer man who should be a servant unto the inner self, for the outer man is limited in time of expression, in period of existence, in capabilities, and endurance.

The outer man attempts to judge the world by his comprehension, and this is but an infinitesimal part of the apprehension on the part of the Divine Self. It is only when the outer man attunes himself with the inner that limited comprehension widens into universal comprehension, and man becomes cognizant of a great world in which he lives. In keeping with this widening of consciousness, there comes an influx of Cosmic Consciousness and Cosmic Attunement, and in this man finds a power and a strength that is beyond any power or energy of the material world.

As I have said above, man tends toward thinking of himself as an individual, separated, isolated, and unique unto himself. By contemplating the Divine Self within, man broadens his consciousness to the extent where he senses and finally realizes that the real part of him is but a part of all of the *real expression* in the universe, and that he is not separated from the rest of mankind and is not an individual, but an inseparable segment of the universal self or soul.

If in a material sense it is true that in union there is strength, and if in our mundane affairs association and cooperation bring added fortitude and security, certainly then in the wider sense the unification of all soul expressions on the earth, and the inseparable association of the real self of man with the real self of all other men, bring security, a power, and a strength that make man the dominating master of his fate and his destiny. But man cannot master his career or his life by considering that he is the skipper of a ship that sails the seas, unrelated to any of the other ships that he passes, or that he knows to exist on the seas of life. Man can no more direct his course in life, independent of any consideration of the other beings, than can one of the comets in the sky arbitrarily select a course for its rapid movement and successfully avoid the collisions and catastrophes that would be inevitable. The success of any man is a joy and a benefit to others, and the failure of any man is a sorrow to all others. Success begets success, as happiness begets happiness and joy. Tolerance, sympathy, and love attune men not only to one another, but to the universal laws, and to the harmony of the Cosmic. Of these *love* is unquestionably the greatest *law* of the universe.

Much is said in the business world of the code of ethics by which business should be standardized in operation, and in the social world we hear of the moral code and the conventions. To the mystic who is attuned with the Cosmic laws there comes a code of principles for living that supersedes the man-made code of ethics or the morals and conventions of society. He learns with conviction and proper understanding why ethics in business and morals, and conventions in society have been established and reduced to definite words by man, and why these things are a necessity. He knows that it is not simply immoral to violate one of Nature's ethical laws, but a sin against himself and against society, as well as a sin against Cosmic decree. Therefore, immorality or the violation of Nature's laws in any sense becomes abhorrent to him.

He realizes that the most beautiful of principles in the universe are reduceable by the undeveloped mind or the evil mind in the physical part of man to corruption and perversion. He realizes that while *love* is the one universal *law* that is higher than all others, it must be a love that is free from the contaminations of the physical self, and free from the sins of lust and selfishness. He realizes that while this great law of life makes it incumbent upon him to love all creatures and all beings, and to love his neighbor as himself, that to reduce this law to the selfish or personal, physical love of the animal part of himself, in an unbridled manner and with promiscuity, is to pervert a divine principle to a coarse and vulgar application.

The laws of Karma and of Cosmic Compensation reveal to him that he cannot do an injustice to another, or take advantage of another, or even live a dual existence, without bringing into his life inevitable suffering and sorrowful adjustment. Hence the mystic's comprehension of ethics and morality has a cleaner and more definite meaning to him, and elicits an obedience to Cosmic Law which man is reluctant to give to a mundane law or the laws of man's invention.

In the home, in business, in society, and in our private personal affairs, man must be true unto himself, and this self must be the inner self, if man is to be true at all. He must let the Divine power within him dominate the physical power of his body and the world around him. He must let the beauty, the grandeur, and the sublime thoughts of the Divine Mind of his being fill him with the inspiration and comprehension of his real place in the universe and of his relationship to all other beings. He must let the God Consciousness of his soul control and direct the health and activities of the physical self so that it may truly be the servant unto him, and not a master whipping him into submission and earthly servility. In this way will man rise to power and glory and attain the highest degree of success and happiness in all of the affairs of the home and of the business world.

INDEX

A

Abilities, latent, 17
Abstractions, speculative, 10
Abundance, 18, 36, 113
Adjustment, 32
Advancement (See Promotion)
Affirmations, 19-37; 151
  Misunderstanding, 29-37
  Mystic, 23
  Negative, 21-25; 33, 35
  Untrue, 19-20
Aid, appealing, 87, 119
Alchemy:
  Mental, 53-59
  Physical, 53
Artist, 74
Attunement, 10, 17, 30, 55,
  116, 187, 225, 230, 232
  Cosmic, 17, 30, 60
Author, 15-17; 155

B

Benedictions, 117
Better business bureaus, 15
Blessing, 37
Board of education, 196
Boards of trade, 15
Books:
  Mastery of Life—AMORC,
    18
  Rosicrucian Principles for
    the Home and Business—
    Lewis, 17
Business clubs and societies,
  15-16
Business guilds, 15
Business magazines, 16
Business, share, 129-130

C

Cause and causes, 20-24;
  32-36
Chance (See Luck)
Character, 95-97
Child of God's love, 24, 32

Child of God's perfect mani-
  festation, 29
Church, 190-194
"Clean hands," 84, 85, 100
Clubs, 15
Coal magnate, 158-159
Coercion by employee, 132
Compensation (See Law of
  compensation)
Competition, 189-190; 206
Concentration, 39-53; 58, 67,
  68, 75, 77, 80, 85-88; 140
  Dr. Lewis' findings, 40
  Fulfillment, 40, 46
  On nose, 152-153
  What to consider, 52
Contentment, 59, 116
Conventions, 232
Corruption, 233
Cosmic:
  Abundance, 29
  Aid, 21-23; 108-114; 151
  Approval, 10
  Blessings, 23, 29
  Commanding and de-
    manding, 61-65
  Compensation (See Law of
    compensation)
  Consciousness, 32, 230
  Contact, 59
  Cooperation, 62, 65, 90, 100
  Decision, 90-92
  Fairness, 84, 92
  Gifts, 79
  Harmony, 219, 232
  Help, 61-78; 87, 91-93;
    100-103; 186
  Honesty and, 84-86
  Law, 23, 61, 171-172; 176,
    186, 187, 217, 219, 232
  Masters, 219
  Petitioning, 113-117
  Power, 54
  Principles, 163, 217-219
  Supply, 186
Cosmic Hosts, 187

Scientific principle, 157
Slapping their heads, 158
Thirteenth, Friday, 157
Walking around chairs, 158
White horse, 157
Supply, abundant, 29, 36-37
Svengali, 153
Sycophancy, 204
Sympathy, 141, 232

T

Talents, dormant, 17
Telepathy, 139, 141, 164-168
Thankfulness, 116
Tolerance, 232
Tombstone, 219
Typing, 74

U

Universal ideas, 29

V

Venetian Theatre, 196, 198
Vibrations, 158, 160
Visualizing, 55-59; 67, 72,
    87-90; 93-94; 139, 146-
    147; 160-165; 190

W

Wealth, 12, 19, 105-117;
    183
    Attainment, 105-109;
        111-117
    Material, 109, 117
Will, 10, 22-24; 31, 36, 58
Women in business, 119-125
Woodbury plan, 176-180
Work, 63-64; 106-108
Wrong, 23

Y

You, 29-38

THE ROSICRUCIAN ORDER
Purpose and Work of the Order

Anticipating questions which may be asked by the readers of this book, the publishers take this opportunity to explain the purpose of the Order and how you may learn more about it.

There is only one universal Rosicrucian Order existing in the world today, united in its various jurisdictions, and having one Supreme Council in accordance with the original plan of the ancient Rosicrucian manifestoes. The Rosicrucian Order is not a religious or sectarian society.

This international organization retains the ancient traditions, teachings, principles, and practical helpfulness of the Order as founded centuries ago. It is known as the *Ancient Mystical Order Rosae Crucis,* which name, for popular use, is abbreviated into AMORC. The headquarters of the English Grand Lodge, AMORC, is located at San Jose, California.

The Order is primarily a humanitarian movement, making for greater health, happiness, and peace in people's *earthly lives,* for we are not concerned with any doctrine devoted to the interests of individuals living in an unknown, future state. The Work of Rosicrucians is to be done *here* and *now*; not that we have neither hope nor expectation of *another* life after this, but we *know* that the happiness of the future depends upon *what we do today for others* as well as for ourselves.

Secondly, our purposes are to enable all people to live harmonious, productive lives, as Nature intended, enjoying *all* the privileges of Nature and all benefits and gifts equally with all of humanity; and to be *free* from the shackles of superstition, the limits of ignorance, and the sufferings of avoidable *Karma.*

The Work of the Order, using the word "work" in an official sense, consists of teaching, studying, and testing such laws of God and Nature as make our members Masters in the Holy

Temple (the physical body), and Workers in the Divine Laboratory (Nature's domains). This is to enable our members to render *more efficient help* to those who do not know, and who need or require help and assistance.

Therefore, the Order is a school, a college, a fraternity, with a laboratory. The members are students and workers. The graduates are unselfish servants of God to humanity, efficiently educated, trained, and experienced, attuned with the mighty forces of the Cosmic or Divine Mind, and Masters of matter, space, and time. This makes them essentially Mystics, Adepts, and Magi—creators of their own destiny. There are no other benefits or rights. All members are pledged to give unselfish service, without other hope or expectation of remuneration than to evolve the Self and prepare for a *greater* Work.

The Rosicrucian Sanctum membership program offers a means of personal home study. Instructions are sent quarterly in specially prepared weekly lectures and lessons, and contain a summary of the Rosicrucian principles with such a wealth of personal experiments, exercises, and tests as will make each member highly proficient in the attainment of certain degrees of mastership. These correspondence lessons and lectures comprise several Degrees. Each Degree has its own Initiation ritual, to be performed by the member at home in his or her private home sanctum. Such rituals are not the elaborate rituals used in the Lodge Temples, but are simple and of practical benefit to the student.

If you are interested in knowing more of the history and present-day helpful offerings of the Rosicrucians, you may receive a *free* copy of the introductory booklet entitled the *Mastery of Life* by calling our toll-free telephone number 1-800-88-AMORC, or by writing to:

Rosicrucian Order, AMORC
1342 Naglee Avenue
San Jose, California 95191, U.S.A.

ROSICRUCIAN LIBRARY

SELF MASTERY AND FATE WITH THE CYCLES OF LIFE
by H. Spencer Lewis, Ph.D., F.R.C.

This book demonstrates how to harmonize the self with the cyclic forces of each life.

Happiness, health, and prosperity are available for those who know the periods in their own life that enhance the success of varying activities. Eliminate "chance" and "luck," cast aside "fate," and replace these with self mastery. Complete with diagrams and lists of cycles.

THE MYSTICAL LIFE OF JESUS
by H. Spencer Lewis, Ph.D., F.R.C.

A full account of Jesus' life, containing the story of his activities in the periods not mentioned in the Gospel accounts, *reveals the real Jesus* at last.

This book required a visit to Palestine and Egypt to secure verification of the strange facts found in Rosicrucian records. Its revelations, predating the discovery of the Dead Sea Scrolls, show aspects of the Essenes unavailable elsewhere.

This volume contains many mystical symbols (fully explained), photographs, and an unusual portrait of Jesus.

COSMIC MISSION FULFILLED
by Ralph M. Lewis, F.R.C.

This illustrated biography of Harvey Spencer Lewis, Imperator of the Ancient Mystical Order Rosae Crucis, was written in response to many requests from Rosicrucians and others who sought the key to this mystic-philosopher's life mission of rekindling the ancient flame of *Wisdom* in the Western world. We view his triumphs and tribulations from the viewpoint of those who knew him best.

Recognize, like him, that the present is our *moment in Eternity*; in it we fulfill our mission.

LEMURIA—THE LOST CONTINENT OF THE PACIFIC
by Wishar S. Cervé

Where the Pacific now rolls in a majestic sweep for two thousand miles, there was once a vast continent known as Lemuria.

The scientific evidences of this lost race and its astounding civilization with the story of the descendants of the survivors present a cyclical viewpoint of rise and fall in the progress of civilization.

THE CONSCIENCE OF SCIENCE and Other Essays
by Walter J. Albersheim, Sc.D., F.R.C.

A remarkable collection of fifty-four essays by one of the most forthright writers in the field of science and mysticism. His frank and outspoken manner will challenge readers to look again to their own inner light, as it were, to cope with the many advances in modern technology.

MANSIONS OF THE SOUL

by H. Spencer Lewis, Ph.D., F.R.C.

Reincarnation—the world's most disputed doctrine! What did Jesus mean when he referred to the "mansions in my Father's house"?

This book demonstrates what Jesus and his immediate followers knew about the rebirth of the soul, as well as what has been taught by sacred works and scholarly authorities in all parts of the world.

Learn about the cycles of the soul's reincarnations and how you can become acquainted with your present self and your past lives.

SECRET SYMBOLS OF THE ROSICRUCIANS
of the 16th and 17th Centuries

This large book is a rare collection of full-size plates of original Rosicrucian symbols and documents. A cherished possession for students of mysticism, this collection includes the Hermetic, alchemical, and spiritual meaning of the unique Rosicrucian symbols and philosophical principles passed down through the ages.

The plates are from originals and are rich in detail. The book is 12" by 18" and is bound in durable textured cover stock.

ROSICRUCIAN QUESTIONS AND ANSWERS WITH COMPLETE HISTORY OF THE ORDER
by H. Spencer Lewis, Ph.D., F.R.C.

From ancient times to the present day, the history of the Rosicrucian Order is traced from its earliest traditional beginnings. Its historical facts are illuminated by stories of romance and mystery.

Dozens of questions in this well-indexed volume are answered, dealing with the work, benefits, and purpose of the Order.

ROSICRUCIAN PRINCIPLES FOR THE HOME AND BUSINESS
by H. Spencer Lewis, Ph.D., F.R.C.

This volume contains the practical application of Rosicrucian teachings to such problems as: ill health, common ailments, how to increase one's income or promote business propositions. It shows not only what to do, but what to avoid, in using metaphysical and mystical principles in starting and bringing into realization new plans and ideas.

Both business organizations and business authorities have endorsed this book.

GREAT WOMEN INITIATES or the Feminine Mystic
by Hélène Bernard, F.R.C.

Throughout history, there have been women of exceptional courage and inspiration. Some, such as Joan of Arc, are well known; others have remained in relative obscurity—until now. In this book, Hélène Bernard examines from a Rosicrucian viewpoint the lives of thirteen great women mystics. Her research and insight have unveiled these unsung heroines who, even in the face of great adversity, have staunchly defended freedom of thought and the light of mysticism.

THE MYSTIC PATH
by Raymund Andrea, F.R.C.

This informative and inspirational work will guide you across the threshold of mystical initiation. The author provides insights into the states of consciousness and experiences you may have as you travel the Mystic Path. It is filled with the fire and paths of the initiate's quest. His spiritual, mental, and physical crises are fully described and pondered. Andrea's deep understanding of the essence of Western mystical and transcendental thought makes this a book you will treasure and refer to often as you advance in your mystical studies. Among the many topics addressed are: Meditation, Contemplation, Awakening Consciousness, the Dark Night of the Soul, Mystical Participation, and Mystical Union.
